LIVES OF
GRIZZLIES

MONTANA AND WYOMING

BY JIM COLE

FOREWORD BY LARRY AUMILLER

FARCOUNTRY
PRESS

HELENA, MONTANA

D1212835

To my parents, Lois and Bob, my all-time best friends, my heroes. They both were always there for me with love, encouragement, good advice, and heartfelt laughter. They would have been so proud to see my books. To my close friends Bill Edelman and Eddy Merle Watson, who have been a daily inspiration to me since their early passing. To my beloved sister, Tootsie. We shared many great adventures together. In fact, we shared our whole lives. I saw my first grizzlies with her, and she was always comfortable in their presence.

Front cover: *Mother and yearlings, Obsidian Creek, Yellowstone National Park*
Back cover: *Female, Yellowstone National Park*

Library of Congress Cataloging-in-Publication Data

Cole, Jim.
    Lives of grizzlies. Montana and Wyoming.
        p. cm.
    ISBN 1-56037-300-8
    1. Grizzly bear—Montana. 2. Grizzly bear—Wyoming. I. Title.
    QL737.C27C635 2004
    599.784'09786—dc22

                                                                2004013435

ISBN 1-56037-300-8
Text and photography © 2004 by James R. Cole
© 2004 Farcountry Press

For more information about our books write Farcountry Press, P.O. Box 5630, Helena, MT 59604; call (800) 821-3874; or visit www.farcountrypress.com.

Created, produced, and designed in the United States.
Printed in Korea.

08   07   06   05   04   1   2   3   4   5

Table of Contents

◀ *Swiftcurrent Valley, Glacier National Park*

Foreword
Lives of Grizzlies: Montana and Wyoming
Lives of Grizzlies: Alaska

Each summer for the past three decades I've guided several hundred people through the McNeil River State Game Sanctuary. Every day our small group of humans passes the day among bears, sometimes as many as seventy. No matter the weather, the number of bears, or the bear activity, the visitors are ecstatic. Their faces light with wonder and sense of awe. I am privileged to witness this vital connection between humans and bears.

Most Americans aren't able literally to walk in the world of bears. Nonetheless, for many people bears are the ultimate symbol of wilderness, and there exists a strong spiritual link between humanity and the natural (non-human) world. Today people generally have high regard for what has been called North America's most visible "charismatic megafauna."

This was not always the case. Non-indigenous North Americans have a long history of persecution of many animals (and peoples) found in the New World. Conservation of animals and their habitat is a relatively new concept, and the idea was germinated in part because so much had been destroyed prior to the twentieth century. *Ursus arctos* (brown and grizzly bears) has been reduced to less than 1 percent of its former range in the contiguous forty-eight states. Even in Canada and Alaska there are populations of bears that are either isolated or scratch for a living in marginal habitat.

In order for our children to be able to live in or visit bear country, we have to get to know bears. First, we need to understand why bears are important. Some comprehension of the importance of bears can be gained second-hand. A simple appreciation of natural history gives us a general sense. For delightful detail, ordinary folks who spend time with bears are willing to tell us their stories and give us their observations. The kind of knowledge I'm speaking about seldom comes from the media—

newspapers, magazines, and most books on bears. For even more detail, wildlife biologists are building a minute record of bear physiology and ecosystem relationships.

Why should we care about bears? It would be a loss not only to humanity but to earth's web of life if bears were reduced or extirpated from parts of their range. One reason to make room for bears that has received lots of attention recently is knowledge about their physiology—information that could someday help humans. Bears are amazingly unique mammals in their ability to carry large amounts of fats into hibernation without apparent negative effects. In the den, they are able to retain urea and not defecate for months. A variety of metabolic changes while in the den and the ability to remain inert for six months without diminished bone density or muscle tone are physiological wonders that could help human medicine in a variety of ways.

Speaking from an ecological view, bears are important as an umbrella species. Bears require a lot of high-quality habitat. This means that, if bears have suitable places to live, then hundreds of other plant and animal species also have suitable homes. Bears are also an indicator species in that they are more sensitive and vulnerable to habitat change than many other species. If bears aren't doing well where they once thrived, it could mean that other species in that environment are at risk too. Also, we are learning that bears can be critical for seed dispersal and nutrient recycling. And when bears act as predators, they play another role in a healthy ecosystem. We are continually learning more about how the web of life works, with bears as major contributors.

Our firsthand experience with bears is equally important for their long-term survival. In an increasingly human-dominated environment, people have to connect viscerally with bears. This connection motivates people to care and to

take action. Action by individuals or a society translates to supportive land use decisions and conservative management of bears.

On a more philosophical level, bears are symbols and reminders. They are the consummate symbol of wilderness in North America. Anyone who's hiked or camped in wilderness with *and without* brown bears can feel the difference. Sharing the ground with a creature as powerful as a grizzly humbles us humans. The existence of bears makes a place wild. At the same time, it fosters sharing and gives modesty and perspective.

I believe that all the knowledge in the world still may not make someone care about bears. Many of us need to experience bears and their environment personally to understand and value them. This means spending time in the bears' world with the bears themselves. But firsthand experience of bears is getting more difficult to attain, because they live on the inaccessible margins of the earth. Increasingly, we see islands of bears in a sea of humanity. Even if a person wants to visit places where bears walk, they are hindered by well-meaning land and wildlife managers afraid that teeming numbers of visitors will displace the bears they come to see.

This is why Jim Cole's two books are important. Jim has worked hard to draw readers into the bears' world at a time when bears need support. Jim has more than magnificent photographs as a result of more than two decades of travels in bear country; he has a deep personal attachment and knowledge of his subjects. Through his eyes, readers live a bear's life, in all its richness, hardships, and triumphs. Jim captures the beauty that exists in the world of the bear, and he shares it with us.

LARRY AUMILLER
Manager, McNeil River State Game Sanctuary
Department of Fish and Game, State of Alaska

Introduction

The wind was howling along the shores of Saint Mary Lake as my sister and I headed west on the few miles of Going-To-The-Sun-Road that remained open to vehicles in early November. A dusting of fresh snow blanketed the very tops of the great pyramid-shaped peaks, and the raging lake was covered with whitecaps. The open, windswept landscape was brutally cold. Needless to say, it was not a good day to hike. We were relegated to sightseeing along the roads. I'd previously spotted two black bears in my entire life, but I yearned to see a grizzly. This was 1975, and I wish I had written down the date. No other cars were around.

Suddenly a beautiful, light brown grizzly bear mother and her two blond furry yearling cubs bolted across the road directly in front of my 1963 Chevy one-ton orange panel truck. They were coming from the lake and headed for cover. When the bears stopped momentarily at the edge of the timber, the mother stood and looked right at us. Then, in a flash, all three scampered into the woods.

The sighting lasted just a few brief seconds but, looking back, this was as close to a life-changing event as I have ever had.

This book is a personal record of my experiences with grizzly bears in their last remaining natural habitats south of the Canadian border. It is for everyone who has seen a wild grizzly, for those who would like to, and for those who care about the future of the great bears and the wild, rugged country where they live. Like the bear following its nose through life from one intriguing smell to another, I have been a keen observer with an intense desire to learn everything I could about grizzly bears. Over the years, I was fortunate to receive an extraordinary gift: the discovery of my life's passion and the ability and tenacity to fol-

low it. It is my privilege to share rare glimpses into the lives of these fascinating creatures.

This book is one of two related volumes that document a wide range of grizzly bear ecosystems in North America. These ecosystems present an excellent cross section but an incomplete representation of grizzly bear habitat and behavior. It simply is not possible to go everywhere and see everything, although I certainly would like to. The companion book, *Lives of Grizzlies: Alaska,* observes bears in seven Alaskan and Yukon ecosystems. The book now in your hands follows the seasonal life cycles of grizzlies in parts of Montana and Wyoming, the last major strongholds of the great bear in the lower forty-eight states. A special chapter in this book gives an intimate, concentrated look at two springs in the life of a memorable grizzly bear family in Yellowstone National Park.

Each ecosystem presents bears a unique set of challenges, including some level of human activity with which the bears must contend. Bears and

people have been sharing these lands for thousands of years. I have found it remarkable that grizzlies can make a living in so many different ways throughout such divergent habitats and seasonal conditions. With every new field season, new observations give me a better appreciation and understanding of their resourcefulness in finding food and adapting to changing environments. I have come to realize that there will always be something new to learn about the bear. The more I study, the more I realize how little I know.

I go to great lengths to document grizzly bear behavior, with my patience being tested constantly. Sometimes I observe bears reacting to other people, but this certainly is not my main focus. It is important to me that my disturbance is minimal. I want to document natural grizzly behavior, not bears reacting to humans. All the same, as careful as I try to be, I certainly have made my share of mistakes.

Wherever possible, I take advantage of viewing opportunities from the road, particularly in

Yellowstone National Park. The majority of the sightings in the Yellowstone and Shoshone National Forest chapters of this book were documented from roads. But my greatest learning has come from hiking in bear country, primarily long day hikes in Yellowstone and Glacier national parks but also many extended backpacking trips. Over the past thirty years, I have hiked thousands of miles of lower forty-eight grizzly country where humans are rarely seen. Although I wasn't very well prepared in the early years, I now always have a camera ready in a hip holster on my left side and binoculars ready in a fanny pack on my right. Most of my photographs are taken without a tripod.

I do not carry a gun in bear country. It is my choice to come into their home and my responsibility to assume the risks. But I always have a can or two of bear spray ready on my belt. I carry extra gear in my backpack in case of emergencies, and sometimes I bring along a light tripod and spotting scope for long-distance observations so I can watch an undisturbed bear for several hours. I use the spotting scope most often from roads. When in grizzly country, I always keep a daily journal. Without it, I could never have written this book.

I have shared many grand adventures, mostly in Glacier National Park, with my good friend Tim Rubbert, a grizzly bear naturalist from Whitefish, Montana. Even with old, trail-battered binoculars, Tim has spotted many a distant grizzly that I never would have seen. He is the only person I know who equals my enthusiasm for the great bear, and it has been said that, when we see grizzlies, "energy bounces between us like electrons between supercharged particles." We each usually hike alone, but we hike together whenever possible. Tim sprayed the bear that attacked me, and he is a great partner on the trail.

Even though I have been mauled by a grizzly (see p. 91), that misadventure neither created

fear nor altered my feeling for bears. I know that this type of encounter is rare, and my attitude has never wavered. This book is a labor of love and is based almost entirely on my firsthand experiences. My accounts are primarily independent observations and are not meant to be technical biology lessons. To avoid drawing more humans into sensitive locations, I purposely withhold the names of some places portrayed in this book. The photographs represent "moments" when I was lucky to be prepared at the right time. Many other opportunities were missed or bungled for one reason or another.

Bears have plenty to contend with in their natural world: unpredictable weather, raging rivers, droughts, fires, avalanches, other bears. But the ever-increasing human intrusion into almost every grizzly bear ecosystem in the lower forty-eight states presents a challenge over which they have no control. Grizzly bears require massive

amounts of wild landscape, and we humans cannot continue to invade and disrupt the wilderness if the grizzly is to survive. We know that grizzlies can adapt to natural environmental change if given the chance. They cannot adapt, however, if they have no place to go. The last wild places must be protected for future generations of bears and humans. We can fight and win a hundred battles to preserve a critical area, but one loss and it is gone forever.

Many people have an irrational fear of grizzlies, fueled by lack of knowledge. They simply don't know much about these physically imposing creatures. Sensational journalism exacerbates the fear and exaggerates the danger, clouding the fact that bear attacks are quite rare. In Yellowstone National Park, for example, the most common causes of human mortality are heart attacks, automobile accidents, drownings, and falls; bear maulings hardly make the list, with only five fatal attacks since 1872. Individuals can have safe, informative, and awe-inspiring experiences in the grizzly bear's country—as long as they take with them an informed and healthy respect for these wonderful creatures.

It is my fervent hope that these two books help people develop exactly that. Grizzly bears are the most interesting and imaginative animals I have ever seen, and my passion for them increases with every year. At a given point in time in different parts of North America, grizzlies could be gorging on a beached whale, chasing ground squirrels in an open field, or engaging in a bout of family wrestling on a remote alpine snowfield. Through my studies I have come to appreciate the whole community of life shared by grizzlies. The great bear is the ultimate symbol of true wilderness and a key barometer of the overall health of an ecosystem. The more folks see and understand these incredible creatures, I believe, the more they will support protection of both the bears and their habitat.

Bear Populations

No more than one hundred years ago, grizzly bears roamed every Western and Plains state. Their range stretched from western Missouri, across the Great Plains and Rocky Mountains, all the way to the Pacific coast. It is about that long since grizzlies have been seen in California, although the great bear still flies on that state flag.

It has been estimated that there are only about a thousand grizzlies in the lower forty-eight today, occupying one to two percent of this historic range. The most significant populations live in and around two large areas: the Greater Yellowstone Ecosystem (GYE) and the Northern Continental Divide Ecosystem (NCDE). The GYE includes Yellowstone and Grand Teton national parks along with seven adjacent national forests.The NCDE includes Glacier National Park, the Rocky Mountain Front, and five national forests. A precious few grizzlies still cling to survival in Idaho, Washington, and the extreme northwest corner of Montana.

My studies in Montana and Wyoming have been focused on important portions of these two major ecosystems. Each offers bears a different set of resources and obstacles. In the GYE, the grizzlies of Yellowstone National Park search for calories throughout big, open valleys and alpine forests. They are the most meat dependent of any known interior grizzly bear population. Heavy tourist traffic on the extensive Yellowstone road system is a special challenge to bears, though it also creates great bear-viewing opportunities. Shoshone National Forest is a rugged mountainous region just east of Yellowstone. Here conflicts between bears and humans have been on the rise. In some years, I have observed grizzlies foraging on a wide variety of rich, seasonal vegetation in this area.

With dramatic scenery throughout and great hiking trails, Glacier National Park is in the heart of the NCDE and is my favorite place in the world. Its lush vegetation and berries are prime

food sources for grizzlies, although the recent multi-year drought has made life difficult for these bruins. The adjacent Rocky Mountain Front supports the last remaining plains grizzlies, some of which are finding food on private lands and coming into conflict with ranchers because of it.

Bear Identification

"Grizzly" and "brown" are different names for the same species, *Ursus arctos*. The populations that thrive in coastal Alaska are normally referred to as brown bears, and these are the main subjects of the second book in this set. For the most part, these coastal bruins are larger than the interior grizzlies of Montana and Wyoming, thanks to abundant salmon. Although each ecosystem has its own characteristics, interior bears are smaller overall because they have no steady source of meat and rely primarily on seasonal vegetation and berries to survive.

The black bear, *Ursus americanus*, is a different species altogether. Do not be confused by the reference to color in the names "brown bear" and "black bear." Either species can be brown, blond, black, white, or anything in between, although some populations tend toward a particular coloration. For example, a high percentage of eastern black bears are black, and many brown bears in the lower forty-eight have a silver tipping on their guard hairs, creating a "grizzled" appearance. An individual bear's color can change seasonally as it loses and grows back its winter coat. And if that isn't confusing enough, lighting conditions and whether a bear is wet or dry also affect appearance.

The best way to distinguish these two species is to look at a bear's physical characteristics, and that is not always easy. The grizzly bear has a concave, dished face, long front claws, and a pronounced shoulder hump. These are indicative but not necessarily useful features; black bears may also show a hump when their head is down, and often a bear's claws are not clearly visible. The black bear has a straight facial profile, much shorter front claws that are well adapted for climbing, and, when viewed from the side, a rump that is usually higher than the shoulders. For the most part, grizzlies are much larger and spend more time in open country than the secretive black bear, but an adult black bear can be much bigger than a young grizzly.

This is just a thumbnail sketch of the physical characteristics, and there are plenty of exceptions. Grizzlies and black bears share the land in Montana and Wyoming, and even the most knowledgeable experts occasionally spot a bear they cannot readily identify. Many grizzlies have been killed by being mistaken for black bears. In the lower forty-eight states, the grizzly bear is listed as a threatened species under the Endangered Species Act, and it is illegal to hunt them. Hunters should never shoot at any bear unless they can make a positive identification, even if it means passing up a good opportunity.

Grizzly Bears	Black Bears

▲ *Facial profiles* ▲

▲ *Claws* ▲

▲ *Shoulders* ▲

Bear Behavior

Grizzlies are intelligent and adaptable. They learn quickly and do not forget. This is a blessing and a curse. The grizzlies of Montana and Wyoming generally do best in terrain that is relatively safe from human access. If a bear learns by experience to avoid humans, its chances for a long life increase. On the other hand, a bear that acquires a taste for human food, garbage, or other non-natural food attractants will usually keep coming back for more and eventually get into trouble.

Grizzly bears have eyesight that is about equal to a human's, hearing that is far superior to ours, and a sense of smell that is unparalleled in the animal kingdom. Although they rely primarily on their noses, they use all three senses to help evaluate situations and courses of action carefully. Each bear is an individual, with its own characteristic temperament and personality. A grizzly that appears passive can become aggressive under the right circumstances—like any of us. These bears have often been typecast as unpredictable, but I believe this reflects our ignorance of them and their signals rather than something about the bears themselves. Most of the time, grizzlies in the lower forty-eight are solitary and secretive and go to great lengths to avoid people and other bears. Socialization can, however, be a significant aspect of their lives, especially when many bears meet and interact at a critical food source like a great huckleberry patch or an army cutworm moth site.

Resourceful omnivores with an uncompromising need for remote undisturbed land, grizzly bears sometimes cover a home range of hundreds of square miles. Their diets vary as much as their surroundings. It's a tough life as they stay on the move, making each decision on the basis of seasonal food availability and risks. Grizzly bears in the lower forty-eight eat berries, flowers, flower bulbs, grasses, sedges, herbs, tubers, leaves, roots, forbs, and nuts. On the carnivorous side, they consume fish, moths, ants, termites, worms, carrion, ungulate (primarily elk and moose) calves,

and rodents. We don't know everything bears eat, but much has been learned from observation and scat collection. It is obvious that bears know more than we humans ever will about wilderness nutrition. When seasonal food sources fail, grizzlies seek alternatives and often expand their range or tap distant memories in the quest for

calories. After several years of drought in Montana and Wyoming, they continue to explore new territory, where conflict with humans is inevitable and tolerance critical. Because of human disturbance in many prime foraging areas, some grizzlies retreat to remote and rugged terrain to settle for secondary food sources.

In a remarkable life cycle suited to the harsh cycle of seasons, most grizzly bear mating occurs from May through July so as not to interfere with the pre-hibernation feeding frenzy called "hyperphagia," which takes place in late summer and early fall. Because of delayed implantation of the

fertilized egg, females give birth in the den during the winter and, for their first few months, newborn cubs live and grow entirely from nursing. The mother bear's fat reserve provides her tiny offspring with all of their nutrition until they emerge from the den in the spring. The length of hibernation varies from year to year, depending on climate, location, food availability, physical condition, age, and gender.

Grizzlies have the second-slowest reproductive rate of any mammal in North America (the musk ox is first). On average females have their first litter at six years old and, in the best circumstances, bring new cubs into the world every three years after that. A female may continue to reproduce into her twenties if she stays healthy. Only a mother bear cares for the cubs, and she generally stays with them for approximately two and a half years before kicking them out so she can start a new family the following year. Sometimes cubs stay with their mothers for one year more or one year less, for reasons unknown to us.

A mother bear teaches her cubs and defends them fiercely for as long as they are with her. Where food is widely dispersed, she leads her brood through a large home range to show them different nutritional options. Much of what she shows them likely is based on her own life experiences and what she was shown by her mother. She may teach them how to hunt elk calves, trout, or ground squirrels and even take them to the best berry patches. When a mother bear reacts defensively and retreats from humans or other bears, the cubs are learning a valuable lesson. If mom is a roadside bear, her cubs may well continue this behavior.

Even under the constant protection and tutelage of their mother, cubs have a high mortality rate. When first out on their own, juvenile bears are extremely vulnerable, and many don't make it. There is no shortage of natural obstacles throughout a grizzly bear's life.

Safety in Bear Country

It is easy to find great places to hike and camp where there are no grizzlies. But to me the forests are empty without them. The whole ecosystem is different and so is the attitude of most humans. Walking in grizzly country is exciting and requires a keen awareness of your surroundings, much more so than in a place void of the great bear. There is obviously no full guarantee of safety in grizzly country. Every person enters voluntarily and does so at his or her own risk. But the risk is hardly as severe as sometimes advertised.

For the most part, grizzly bears fear humans and want nothing to do with us. They have a natural desire to live in peace. These physically superior animals could easily attack us often, but they don't. The few attacks that do occur are almost all defensive. They usually happen when bears are surprised or when they are defending a food source or protecting cubs. Such attacks result in varying degrees of injury to humans but are seldom fatal. A grizzly bear's aggression usually subsides when its target is no longer a perceived threat, and this is why it is recommended that you not fight or struggle if attacked. Of course, this is easier said than done.

Individuals have a variety of choices about how to hike in grizzly country. Some talk, sing, wear bells, yell, or blow airhorns to make sure they don't take a bear by surprise. Some stay quiet. I don't like bells because they are perceived as a sure-fire protector and, very often, the folks who wear them lose awareness of their surroundings. "Bear bells" and other noise makers may prevent us from hearing the moose or bear moving nearby through the underbrush. Often I have not heard the bells until I was very close to the source, and so a bear might not hear them either. While giving a false sense of security, they may also scare away the wildlife that some hikers want to see.

To avoid surprising a bear, talking and occasional yelling can be effective, depending on the

circumstances. I prefer not to make constant noise, but that is only my own style. My experience tells me in which situations to vocalize, and I usually make plenty of noise when hiking in dense timber or other places of limited visibility. Hunters walk a fine and risky line when they stalk quietly through the woods—hoping to sneak up on game but also hoping not to stumble onto an unsuspecting grizzly bear.

If you do spot a bear, remember: don't yell, don't make any quick movements, don't run, don't panic. Watch the bear and evaluate the circumstances. Each situation is different, and there are no set rules except to use common sense. If the bear is unaware of your presence, you may want to back away slowly and leave. I usually stand my ground and try not to lose sight of the animal. When a bear does see you, it will often make a swift exit. If it charges, you cannot sprint or climb fast enough to get away.

A bear can run in excess of thirty-five miles per hour—considerably faster than a world class 100 meter sprinter. Most charges by bears are only bluffs, and standing your ground is generally the best idea. Any attempt to escape may turn a bluff charge into a real one.

Even with an increasing number of people venturing out into grizzly country every year, attacks by bears remain rare. All the same, it is only sensible to take all the precautions you can, and carrying bear spray is a good one. Nothing is one hundred percent effective, but time and time again bear spray has worked. It's cheap insurance and more effective than a gun.

Still, knowledge and precautions can take you only so far. Some folks are just so naturally frightened by the thought of encountering a bear that they could never relax and enjoy walking in grizzly country. It's not for everybody. But a good grizzly bear picture book is. Or two of them.

Yellowstone National Park

As afternoon shadows began to lengthen across the narrow, lush meadow, a dark male grizzly led his blond girlfriend out of the forest directly to a cow elk carcass that lay in the mud at the edge of a thermal pond. He forced her to wait nearby as he fed alone. She made several testing approaches with her head down and cocked to the side in a submissive posture. Each time, he made low-pitched growls until she retreated. Although the two bears were about the same size, the male was clearly in control at this time.

Mating pair, south of Twin Lakes ▶

After a half hour he permitted her first bite. They fed together briefly, then he wandered toward a nearby lake and she gorged alone. After another twenty minutes, she joined him at the lake, but they soon returned for a few more bites. A scraggly coyote circled the scene carefully and stole scraps when the bears weren't looking.

It was fascinating to watch the pair reverse roles as they began to move away after the feeding session. Now it was the male who followed, in classic grizzly bear courting behavior, with his powerful nose close to the ground breathing in every bit of her female aroma. He continued behind as they retreated back into the shadows.

The next day a ghostlike figure fed alone in the early morning fog. It had been less than eleven hours since I saw him follow the female into the forest. There was no way of knowing how long they had been together or why the courtship ended. Some mating grizzlies stay together for weeks, others only briefly. For all I know, this pair could have been together for some time and already copulated. Or maybe she didn't like his behavior the night before and went off abruptly in search of another beau. In any case, the male was long gone before the fog lifted, though he returned again that evening for one more meal. Today he had to share only with coyotes and ravens.

Habitat

Yellowstone is perhaps the most unusual and diverse ecosystem of all grizzly homes. It does not resemble any other bear country I have seen, and my early impressions were that it simply did not look like grizzly bear habitat. Although over 75 percent of the park is covered by forest and burned areas, much of the landscape consists of dry, open valleys dominated by sagebrush.

As in all grizzly country, the bruins here consume a wide variety of vegetation throughout their seasonal travels, including biscuitroot, yampa, sedge, bulbs of spring beauties, glacier lilies, roots of various plants, clover, elk thistle, berries, and dandelions. But the vegetation is not lush like it is in Glacier National Park, and berries are seldom abundant. The first Yellowstone grizzly I ever saw was excavating the burrows of pocket gophers in the dry sagebrush. I have since watched many grizzlies moving through the open sagebrush country routinely searching for pocket gopher caches and digging roots.

Aside from these opportunistic finds, Yellowstone grizzlies depend primarily on four major food sources: elk and bison, cutthroat trout, army cutworm moths, and whitebark pine nuts.

Yellowstone is often referred to as the "Serengeti of North America" because of the large elk and bison herds that roam throughout the park. It's easy to see why the Yellowstone grizzly is the most meat dependent of any known interior bear in North America. When grizzlies emerge from hibernation in the spring, they search for winter-killed ungulates, primarily bison and elk. How many they find depends on the harshness of the winter.

From about late May to early July, bears prey heavily on newborn elk calves, which are not yet strong enough to outrun them. Grizzlies have been known to kill bison calves, but there is little docu-

▲ Pelican Valley

▲ Yampa stems

▲ Carrion

▲ Cutthroat trout

mentation and one can only speculate about how often this occurs. In late summer, bison go into the rut and fighting bulls are often weakened or killed. After weighing the risk, grizzlies will either challenge a weakened animal or wait for it to die.

Overall, elk cow–calf ratios have been down over the past three years, and the northern Yellowstone elk herd is estimated to be less than half of what it was ten years ago. In addition, the bison population has fluctuated dramatically in the past few years. The harsh winter of 1996/97 provided abundant carrion for grizzlies, but more than a thousand bison migrated to milder conditions outside park boundaries and were shot or sent to slaughter, and the bison population plummeted. It is feared that these big ungulates carry brucellosis, a disease that threatens domestic cattle. Currently, any bison outside the park that tests positive for brucellosis is destroyed. Although the population has rebounded to near record numbers since 1997, these buffalo may again be subjected to mass execution during another severe winter. Park management policies are constantly evolving in the search for a solution.

Ungulate protein may be available to bears at any time from these and other sources including, to a much lesser extent, moose, deer, antelope, and bighorn sheep. Grizzlies assertively hijack many wolf kills and sometimes finish up the scraps when wolves abandon a carcass. At the same time, it is also becoming more common to see grizzlies being driven away from carrion by large, aggressive wolf packs.

In early summer, many grizzlies feed on spawning cutthroat trout in more than sixty shallow streams that flow into Yellowstone Lake. Today the cutthroat populations are being threatened by alien lake trout introduced illegally. Not only do the more aggressive lake trout consume the cutthroats, but they also spawn in deeper waters and are virtually inaccessible to bears. Efforts are being made to control the lake trout, but the job is a difficult one and the cutthroat food source is at risk.

Later in the summer, grizzlies consume large quantities of protein-rich army cutworm moths on high-elevation talus slopes. The moths migrate hundreds of miles from eastern prairies to consume alpine flower nectar in these remote areas. Grizzlies turn over rocks and lick up thousands of unsuspecting moths. Unfortunately, these moths have not proved to be a dependable food source. Good years and poor ones can come at any time and, although climatic changes are thought to be a factor, the precise reasons are a mystery. Further complicating the situation, some people on the prairies consider these moths pests and spray them with insecticides.

Whenever whitebark pine nuts are abundant, grizzlies retreat to the remote high country in late summer and fall to feed on them. This important food is a highly concentrated source of protein and fat, which bears need before denning. Grizzlies usually obtain the nuts by raiding red squirrel caches. These pine nuts are such a preferred food for grizzlies that, after a "bumper crop" year, some bears eat overwintered pine

nuts in the spring and continue to consume old pine nuts throughout the summer and even into the fall if the current year's crop fails—as it sometimes does. It is obvious that these tiny nuts play a major role in the lives of many Yellowstone grizzlies. In most years of poor nut production, bears generally frequent mid and low elevations in the fall searching for secondary foods.

Unfortunately, this food source has long been threatened by white pine blister rust, a fungus

that kills trees. The disease is rapidly infecting whitebark pines and continues to spread. It has already wiped out the whitebarks in Glacier National Park, leaving those bears one less nutritional option. Based on the Glacier experience alone, the future looks bleak for whitebark pines. To make matters worse, these trees are also now being ravaged by mountain pine beetles. Most experts believe that it's just a matter of time before the whitebark is eliminated from the Yellowstone ecosystem.

All of these threatened food sources are critical to grizzly bears. The threats are mostly connected to human activities, and some parts of the park have seasonal restrictions and closures to limit human intrusion and its effects. The ecosystem may not be able to support current bear populations if their diverse food base is not sustained. It seems likely that, as their sources of food dwindle, Yellowstone bears will expand their travels. New roads built in the surrounding forest service land will add additional stress to the bears. Based strictly on numbers, the Yellowstone bears have been doing well in the past several years. Still, the number of grizzlies at a particular time does not necessarily measure grizzly bear survival. The current and future quality of the habitat determines the long-term health of the population.

Grizzlies and Wolves Compete

At first light the bear walked purposefully through the crusty snow along Slough Creek, with several wolves lurking nearby. Although a bit lean after the long winter, this massive bruin appeared to be in excellent condition. It was March 13, 2001, the earliest grizzly I have ever personally seen. (In a rare sighting almost two months earlier, Cliff Browne, a local photographer from Cook City, Montana, filmed a grizzly digging in the snow.) Ravens and a bald eagle circled around and, with coyotes waiting in the distance, the bear disappeared behind a low ridge heading toward a carcass that was out of my view. After about an hour the dark grizzly emerged, followed closely by five wolves. As he continued to walk steadily away, the bear looked back over his shoulder toward the wolves several times but never stopped moving. Three wolves dropped out of the procession, but two continued pursuing the bear until they were about a half mile from the carcass. When last seen, the bear was gaining elevation as he traveled far to the north. It really looked like the wolves had escorted him away from the area.

I'll never know what went on at the carcass site, but this observation caused me to wonder. Grizzlies often walk right in and take control of wolf kills. But after being worked over by twenty-six wolves, how much could have been left on this particular carcass, and was it worth fighting for? I did see two wolves come away from the kill site with big chunks of meat in their mouths after the bear exited. Though possibly lethargic this early in the year, grizzlies are always hungry. Still, calories are not nearly as important to them now as in the late summer and fall. Can a wolf pack of this size actually dominate a big grizzly? This may depend on who wants the food more. There is obvious strength in numbers. Would the outcome have been different in September or October?

A similar event occurred just across the road below Specimen Ridge. Cliff Browne showed me footage of filming he did on September 25, 2000. A smaller adult grizzly was persistently harassed by this same wolf pack (twenty-seven wolves at that time) as it headed toward a carcass. When the bear moved forward, the wolves would cut it off. They chased the bear around in circles, continually preventing it from proceeding to the kill site. Bears are quick and fast, but they are not as agile as wolves. The canines must be careful because one swipe from a powerful bear paw could mean death. The wolves worked as a team, confusing and biting at the bear from all sides until it retreated in frustration without ever getting near the carcass.

It was late April, and early morning rain began to fall as a dark grizzly moved steadily to the south through Swan Lake Flats with his nose intently sniffing the air. The big bruin suddenly broke into a dead run for several hundred yards. After this long sprint, he stopped at an elk carcass near the south end of Swan Lake. He turned the carcass over and immediately began to feed. The bear then found a second elk carcass close by and turned it over. I could also see a bison horn sticking up, but I could not tell how many carcasses were out there at this one spot. The two elk carcasses I could clearly see appeared to be mostly intact. They were discolored with very little fur, indicating that the bodies were probably old and had possibly been submerged for a while.

Meanwhile, a single gray wolf moved in, wanting a piece of the action. The wolf approached several times and came very close, but the bruin stood his ground. Finally the wolf moved away and the bear fed alone.

The following morning was much colder, with three inches of fresh wet snow on the ground. The same grizzly was obviously on edge as he fed at the carcass site surrounded by five wolves. He abruptly stood and looked all around, then slowly moved away from the site while peeking back over his shoulder. The big bruin then broke out into a dead run, followed by two of the wolves. The bear was long gone by 7:00 A.M. as the five wolves continued their feast.

Springtime

As light snow fell on a late April afternoon, these two sub-adult grizzlies were being chased by a group of bison near Specimen Ridge. The bears worked their way around the herd to a bison carcass and began to feed. They looked around often and stood up several times to check on their larger adversaries. I watched through my spotting scope as one bear lifted the carcass twice but, with poor visibility, it was hard to tell how much meat was left. Finally the bison herd aggressively approached the young grizzlies, who immediately lumbered several hundred yards to cover. It looked like this herd was trying to protect a dead comrade.

It was May 3 and the road through Hayden Valley had just opened for the season at 8:00 A.M. In a typical Yellowstone scene at a thermal area across from Mud Volcano, this big grizzly immediately began to move away when he sensed the presence of humans. He sniffed and looked back while heading straight for the timber. Most adult male bears are shy, and this guy was no exception. It is likely that this particular bear is observed by humans only rarely, and such avoidance behavior will help him to a long, productive life.

After a heavy, wet spring snow-storm, Tim Rubbert and I watched a lone grizzly digging in the snowy sagebrush west of the park road in Hayden Valley. The bear came up to the road and tried to cross, but it balked when startled by a passing truck. The grizzly quickly spun around, then loped away from the road, kicking up fresh snow with every step. At first the bear was just retreating from the roadside commotion. He had no idea that he was headed in the wrong direction, but this would prove to be a very lucky break. As he angled to the northwest toward Alum Creek, his powerful nose picked up the scent. In short order, this grizzly stumbled onto a bison that apparently had died during the night. Photographers told me that they had been watching this weak buffalo stagger around for a few days.

The bear gorged all day as snow returned in the afternoon. He often lifted and repositioned the meat to get at the best sections. He took lengthy naps lying on top the carrion, but I'm sure he slept with one eye open. After every meal and before each nap, he reburied the carcass to hide its smell from other predators—each time moving farther away to find fresh dirt and snow. Had the human disturbance not prevented him from crossing the road, this lucky bear would likely have missed this bonanza altogether.

T he morning was windy and cold with precious few patches of sunlight. It was early spring, and most of the surrounding area was still buried in snow. There were a few small green meadows near the rising smoke at Steamboat Point, a thermal area along the north shore of Yellowstone Lake. I spotted a young grizzly grazing in one of these meadows as a few vehicles pulled over to watch. The bruin showed little reaction to the small human gathering until a loud diesel truck pulled up. The bear gazed anxiously toward the noise, then stood up to look around. Apparently this sub-adult determined that there was no imminent danger, quickly dropped back down to all fours, and calmly resumed munching on sedges and grass. When a bear stands on its two hind legs, it is usually just checking out the surroundings by getting a better look and smell before deciding how to react. This is generally not an aggressive posture.

The wind was whipping the rising thermal smoke, and the smell of sulphur wafted through the air as two bison bulls approached from the west. The grizzly stood and took one long look toward the bison, then bolted across the road between several parked cars. For-tunately, the humans were behaving; everyone was in or behind a vehicle.

The bruin stopped on a muddy hillside across the road and watched the huge ungulates walk slowly into the lush meadow. The bear kept a close eye on them while finding some green forage interspersed in the mud. The bison now controlled the prime meadow, and the bear was probably uncomfortable sharing it with them. The previous day my friend Tim Rubbert had seen a grizzly in this same meadow foraging very close to some bison. We later compared our photographs, and this was the same bear. The unpredictable thought processes of grizzlies never cease to amaze me. I had watched this bear for about an hour when, for no apparent reason, it suddenly galloped up into the trees and disappeared.

From what I have observed over many years, bison and grizzlies coexist extremely well in Yellowstone, especially in the open valleys where they can see the entire area all around them. I've seen bears cautiously approach bison, and vice versa. Most often these two large creatures seem to ignore each other, but I am sure that each is constantly keeping track of the other.

On an overcast day in early spring, a young grizzly had been eating grasses all after-noon at Mary Bay when he approached a dead tree, seemingly curious. After half-heartedly bouncing up and down on the long log several times, he got serious and easily rolled it over, pushing it downhill with his powerful front paws. He briefly licked around for insects but didn't seem to find much. He then sat on the repositioned log for a while, just sniffing the air.

Sagebrush Bear

Late April, and this is the only time I have
seen a bear munch on the long, brownish
tops of sagebrush shrubs.

When this lanky bear wandered through springtime greenery in the grassy meadow, a pesky coyote cautiously followed. The grizzly was digging for rodents, and the crafty canine hung around and pounced on the ones that escaped. Both animals were hunting successfully. I've watched bears get very frustrated trying to chase these agile opportunists. This grizzly was tolerant and apparently decided against wasting energy with futile attempts to discourage the coyote. The unlikely duo continued this activity for over two hours and even took a nap close to each other near a thermal area.

On this cloudy, cool morning the last of the winter snow was still melting near Yellowstone Lake. A pair of sandhill cranes approached as a grizzly began to dig in the open meadow. The small adult bear went about her business and seemed to ignore the cranes. Though the big birds lingered surprisingly close, the busy bruin made absolutely no attempt to chase them away. I suspected that the sandhills were looking for insects, worms, or other scraps unearthed by the bear's fresh diggings, but they did not appear to do any feeding for the entire time I watched. Maybe the bear wasn't digging up what the cranes liked. I had never seen sandhill cranes hover this close to a bear. They nearly walked a complete circle around the seemingly oblivious grizzly. After a while, the cranes and bear casually walked away in opposite directions through the meadow, which subsequently looked naked without them.

A bison carcass had washed up near the shore of the Yellowstone River near Le Hardy's Rapids. A grizzly found it and gorged for a few days, alternating dinner sessions with naps on the shore and in the nearby timber. The same two white pelicans swam by every half hour or so while I watched the bruin feed. Several times, I actually saw the pelican pair float down the river and then fly back up river over my head. They would casually reappear, heading right past the bear along the same route.

Cub Mortality

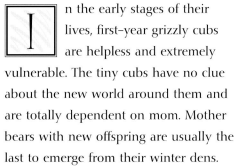

I n the early stages of their lives, first-year grizzly cubs are helpless and extremely vulnerable. The tiny cubs have no clue about the new world around them and are totally dependent on mom. Mother bears with new offspring are usually the last to emerge from their winter dens.

The earliest I have seen cubs of the year was May 13, 2002, and these two had likely been away from their den for only a short time. This bear family spent spring nights on a cliff ledge just below the top of the highest ridge to the north, where the mother bear apparently felt most secure with a great panoramic view. Each day she brought the cubs down the mountain to feed on succulent greenery near Soda Butte Creek. In the process, they weaved their way through tourists and photographers gathered along the roadside. They also had to contend with unsuspecting bison, these huge imposing beasts that the cubs had never seen before. The mother often took her tiny offspring swimming so they could all forage on the far side of Soda Butte Creek. She could easily walk across the creek, but the cubs were forced to paddle through the current. The young ones usually waited nervously on the far shore until mom coaxed them across or came back to them. The creek was getting higher and swifter

each day. These two little ones would have to learn fast.

The most ominous threat to the cubs may have been the resident wolf pack that roamed these hills; the bear family was sleeping and foraging within a half mile of the wolf den. In the early morning of May 14, before the bears came down from their rocky perch, I watched three wolves walk past them along the top of the ridgeline. The night of May 18 was the last time these three bears were seen together. The mother bear was spotted the next day with only one cub, and I saw the pair a couple of days later. I don't know what happened to the other cub, but wolves are high on the list of suspects. It can be emotional for me to look at pictures of these two petite siblings, knowing that one of them had such a short life. I hope the surviving cub will be around for a long time.

Elk Calf Predation

Grizzlies display a distinct behavior when hunting elk calves in the spring. With noses to the ground, bears are often seen relentlessly zigzagging through the sagebrush. Newborn elk calves are thought to have no odor and must be a challenge for a grizzly's nose. Their best defense is to remain motionless and hope the bear passes them by. Nervous mother elk are often seen prancing around trying to divert the bears, but their actions may in fact be alerting them. When a helpless young calf panics and tries to run from a bear, it's all over. The window of opportunity is, however, short. Once healthy calves are about three weeks old, they can usually outdistance a grizzly.

Cow elk often hide their newborn calves in pockets of fallen trees. As this worried mother elk looked on, a grizzly scoured the area. I observed for quite a while, and the frustrated bruin never did find the calf. He finally left empty-handed and still hungry. This often happens when an experienced cow elk finds a good hiding place and the calf remains still.

And sometimes the bear succeeds. A small group of anxious cow elk stood nearby as this big grizzly methodically checked out every smell while he stalking through a burned area just below the park road near Mount Washburn. The bear suddenly lifted his head, with a struggling elk calf in his mouth. The calf screamed as the powerless mother elk looked on in silent agony. It took just over an hour for the grizzly to consume his kill about forty yards from the roadway. Numerous onlookers gathered, creating a "bear jam," but the grizzly did not react to the humans. Only a few bones remained when Tim Rubbert and I inspected the site the next day.

June Separation

The bright afternoon sun shimmered off their magnificent silver-tipped coats as these bears dug in the sagebrush west of the park road near Sheepeater Cliffs. They seemed uneasy with the increasing human activity and stood up several times to check out various noises. The trio slowly moved to the west as they crossed the Gardiner River, then vanished into the forest near Indian Creek Campground. This was May 27, 2002, the first time I saw this mother bear with her two yearling cubs.

Two afternoons later, the bears were in the same spot. That morning, I had seen a newborn elk calf gingerly leaving the area with its mother. The after-birthing smells may have lingered. The mother bear thoroughly sniffed and licked all around as the cubs frolicked nearby. The next day, May 30, was the last time I saw this bear family together.

On June 1, Tim Rubbert watched this bear family nurse on a patch of snow. Some folks told me they saw these three bears the next morning with an adult male grizzly nearby. Even though the mother bear had nursed her cubs the previous afternoon, she may quickly have gone into estrus and run off with a male suitor. This is the likely scenario, because on the evening of June 2, as the dark rainy skies produced an early dusk, Tim and I saw the yearlings alone climbing up the highest bluff on the north end of Swan Lake Flats. This is the latest I have seen cubs kicked out by the mother in this ecosystem, but I don't believe that the timing is unusual. I have known the exact date of separation only a few times. I'm sure it depends on many factors peculiar to the bears that we humans have little comprehension of. We can speculate all we want, but I believe that each situation is unique—just as it is with human separations.

Over the next few weeks, I watched the two yearlings spend much of their time foraging in the open sagebrush on the north end of Swan Lake Flats. I'm sure they were selecting a variety of vegetation, but I specifically saw them mostly digging biscuitroot, and one time they were eating spring beauty flowers. Grizzlies commonly dig up spring beauty bulbs later in the year, but this was the first time I had seen a bear eat the flowers. I watched the two bears pass by elk cows with small calves a few times without any noticeable interest. Maybe they had not seen their mother kill many calves, or perhaps they didn't have the confidence to try it on their own.

As independent yearlings, they were now the lowest bears in the pecking order, and the two were sticking very close together. Their movements were fairly predictable to me for a while as they returned regularly to familiar spots, probably places their mother had taken them. As the temperatures warmed into the 70s, they took more naps on snowfields. They easily found snow patches out in the open with good visibility, thereby killing three birds with one stone: cooling off, resting, and scanning the countryside for impending danger all at the same time. They approached me with seeming curiosity a couple of times while I observed their behavior.

I saw the two siblings for the last time on June 20. As the sun dipped below the brilliant snowy peaks of the Gallatin Range to the west, the young bears walked across a distant hillside, dropped down, and disappeared into the shadows.

Summer Scenes

During the summer, this young grizzly was often seen grazing on the steep hillsides in the meadows north of Dunraven Pass. On June 12, the bear was eating grass in a field of colorful wildflowers highlighted by brilliant shooting stars at their peak. The meadow continued down to a bluff just above the park road, where the bear foraged briefly. As more people congregated at this spot, the bruin gradually began to move away and was soon out of sight. This part of the road had just opened for the season, and the young bear may have been foraging in peace for a few days before the sudden tourist arrival.

This hot August day in Hayden Valley a small dark grizzly traveled along the eastern shore of Yellowstone River. At one point the bear turned abruptly and leaped playfully into the river, chasing mallard ducks that escaped easily. For about twenty minutes the bear turned over rocks on a steep embankment. While hiking I have frequently seen evidence of rock rolling, but this bear was just across the river and I had never seen the behavior so vividly. The bear would roll a rock, quickly lick the insects underneath, then go on to the next rock to repeat the process. Napping and swimming rounded out the bear's routine.

While hiking the wide-open Yellowstone backcountry, I often perch myself on a high point to observe grizzly bear behavior quietly. This way I can usually keep track of the bears and avoid startling them at close range. I've learned that, once I spot a bear, it's easy to lose sight of it while walking through the low rolling hills, and I can never be sure in which direction a bruin is going when it is out of my view.

Most bears never come near, but these grizzlies walked by and carefully checked me out. One mother kept a sharp eye on me with her two tiny cubs close behind. On another day, a curious grizzly mom stood to look me over. Another time, a mother bear looked in my direction while her cub stood and watched. Unless there is carrion close by,

I never feel threatened when I come across grizzlies in these areas. The bears do not feel cornered in the open valleys and can easily move away in almost any direction, except toward me, of course. After they determined that I was not a threat, all of these bear families calmly continued their daily travels. I have never seen a bear act aggressively in such circumstances.

Agile Grizzlies

Bears are agile and athletic. Here a mother bear casually leaped over Elk Antler Creek as her reluctant spring cubs waited behind.

Another mother bear performed her own version of tightrope walking. With her small cub close behind, she gracefully negotiated this narrow log to get across a creek.

Amid gathering onlookers near Lake Butte Overlook, this sub-adult slithered under a fallen tree.

Preparing for Winter

In the fall, grizzly bears often look passive and calm as they meander methodically among bison in the vast Yellowstone valleys. In general, grizzlies do a lot of sniffing and digging. But their demeanor changes markedly when they scare up pocket gophers. Their senses instantly shift to high alert. Their confused faces look intense as they cock their heads back and forth like curious dogs. Mighty grizzlies seem to be in a state of bewilderment as they try to pounce on scurrying rodents who are rapidly escaping in all directions. The bears often can't decide which way to go. I have know idea how successful grizzlies' gopher hunting is because the gophers are small and disappear quickly—whether consumed or down their holes to safety is hard to tell.

Grizzly Crossing

It was a constant struggle in the blowing snow as I watched this grizzly walking along the shore of an open creek in early November. Ice had formed along the edges of the creek, but it still flowed. The bear located the only frozen spot I could see and carefully tiptoed across.

resh snow covered the ground and the temperature was dropping as I watched this young bear make what was probably her last stand of the year near Yellow— stone Lake. For the third time in six days, she was digging up the same row of moist, rocky soil. Each time, she dug the same spots all the way to the end of the row. When she finished, it looked like a gardener had meticulously shaped the soil into neat little mounds. Her feeding was so intense that she paid little attention to the human spectators. The few times she lifted her head, there was often snow on her nose and tubers or yampa stems in her mouth. After a cold horizontal snowstorm blew in at the end of October, I did not see her again.

t was a bumper year for whitebark pine nuts, and with the mild weather many grizzlies were probably still feasting in the high country. As I hiked through a magnificent valley in early November, the bulky grizzly guarding the mound in the snow stuck out like a sore thumb. A six-point elk antler protruded upward from the pile of dirt, giving the bear a convenient scratching post. Two other grizzlies circled the area as the large male swiveled in the mud on top of the carcass to keep tabs on everything around him. Each bear approached the carcass separately, but the big guy faced them off every time and never budged. These

bears all may have been feeding on pine nuts a long way from here when the smell from this huge hunk of carrion lured them in.

Early the next day, one of the other bears inadvertently headed directly toward my hiding spot as he snuck around through the nearby trees. When the bruin spotted me, I didn't move. The dark grizzly took one long look before making a sharp right turn, walked peacefully up the hill, and disappeared into the forest. I was sorry to disturb the hungry bruin, but I probably didn't affect his chances of having elk steak for dinner anytime soon.

With the wind in my face and sun at my back, I silently watched and photographed the drama from the cover of nearby trees. I was constantly looking all around. It was there that I discovered the crusted tracks of at least five wolves leading away from the scene. They may have made the kill. I didn't know how old the

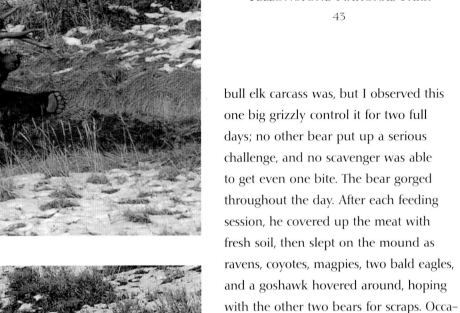

bull elk carcass was, but I observed this one big grizzly control it for two full days; no other bear put up a serious challenge, and no scavenger was able to get even one bite. The bear gorged throughout the day. After each feeding session, he covered up the meat with fresh soil, then slept on the mound as ravens, coyotes, magpies, two bald eagles, and a goshawk hovered around, hoping with the other two bears for scraps. Occa-sionally, when the coast was clear, the feasting bear moved just a few feet from his prize to defecate or eat snow.

When I arrived on the third day, the whole scene had changed. The antlers were completely repositioned above the ground, and it looked to me like most of the meat was gone. Soon thereafter, the big male made a slow exit, and two coy-otes immediately moved in behind him. By this time, the pickings must have been slim. The canines munched a little on the bones but didn't stay around for long.

Temperatures had dipped below zero for the past week as this young grizzly came down to an old bison carcass near the Slough Creek road in the bright sunshine at 10:45 A.M. on November 8. Coyotes had been patrolling the area earlier this morning, but there wasn't much left. A friend told me that wolves had been feeding on it for the past few days. The bear picked at the carcass and found a few scraps but stayed around only for about twenty minutes before exiting over the ridge to the northwest.

The bruin walked a short way on the Slough Creek road, then crossed it, traveling toward the mostly frozen creek. The small bear was heading in the direction of a large bison herd before it detoured around them to the south. The wary bruin then walked around a low ridge and circled back up behind the bison, heading away to the north. A few bison watched, but none of them seemed concerned. It was interesting to watch this young bruin completely avoid the bison herd by making a wide circle around them.

The bear was far off in the distance when it disappeared from my view at 12:15 as the day was warming up. Food was scarce now and this bear may have been on a non-stop journey toward the winter den. Tracks left in the skiff of snow on the Slough Creek road confirmed what a small bear this was.

The latest grizzly I have seen was on November 25, 2000, two days after Thanksgiving. The first snow came early that fall, but the weather had been dry and very cold ever since. The young bruin was munching an elk carcass on the frozen Lamar River right out in the open near the park road. I arrived at about 2:00 P.M. and was told that the pack of twenty-seven wolves had made the kill and was feeding early that morning. The wolves were resting far to the south when the bear came down from the slopes to the north, crossed the road, and claimed the prize. Bear food is scarce this time of year, and most grizzlies were probably in their dens. There wasn't much left, but the

bear was lifting it off the ground, ripping it apart, and consuming every possible morsel. One wolf returned alone but did not challenge the bear. A mature bald eagle perched just a few yards away. Bold coyotes in close proximity shared parts of the carcass. The bear became irritated with the coyotes and chased them off a couple of times, but they would always return when he resumed feeding, and the bear finally decided that it was easier to coexist. At one point he walked about fifty yards away, rolled and played on the snow–covered river, then took a short nap. He wasn't gone long, but the coyotes had the carcass all to themselves until he returned.

Late in the afternoon, the wolves cautiously filtered back into the area and the coyotes made a hasty retreat. In the fading light, three wolves marched right up to the carcass and fed near the grizzly while at least fifteen other wolves reacted to automobile noise by backing away from the riverbank. The three wolves continued to pick at the remaining bones, and the bear decided that it was time to leave. He tried to go back across the road but was cut off by passing cars and twice retreated. More wolves were coming down to the kill site as darkness descended.

Shoshone National Forest

I t was early June as three dark forms emerged from the shadows at the forest's edge in the twilight. This was the first time I saw this radio–collared mom with her two small cubs foraging near the highway. She seemed reasonably comfortable with constant "bear jams." Traffic came to a complete halt whenever they crossed the road, often maneuvering through a maze of bear watchers. With all this commotion, I never saw the mother bear show any aggression toward people.

The following spring she returned with two good–looking yearlings and resumed her pattern of grazing in the road corridor. She was a small female and the cubs appeared small for their age. Tim Rubbert and I were hiking on May 9 when we spotted the three bears moving along a high ridgeline far to the east. They were foraging and doing nothing out of the ordinary, so we watched them for a few minutes, then resumed our walk.

◀ *Spring cubs spar, north fork Shoshone River*

About an hour later we could see the same spot from a different vantage point. Two grizzly bears were mating and, silhouetted on the skyline, the bear on the bottom had an open space on its neck that looked suspiciously like a radio collar. If this was the same mother bear, it surprised us to see her mating. Her cubs were still yearlings, and this seemed like an abrupt separation. Just that morning we had watched them feeding near the road, and a family breakup at this time was the farthest thing from our minds.

We later learned that, in this ecosystem, it is not uncommon for a mother grizzly to kick out yearlings instead of keeping them for the more normal two-year weaning period. I haven't come across information on survival rates for independent yearling grizzlies in this area. If long-term survival is high, the population would be enhanced by such early separations because the reproductive cycle would be shorter and more offspring could be produced. But with one less year of mom's tutelage and a consequent increase in mortality, the overall effect might not be favorable. Yearlings would generally be smaller and far less experienced than two-year-olds.

In the early afternoon, our suspicions were confirmed when we saw the two cubs foraging by themselves. With their

mother out of the picture, these young bears were now tentative and insecure. Within a few days of the breakup, I twice saw the mother alone, right across the road from her cubs. They never came together.

The timid pair actually became a nuisance. They were creating constant traffic problems by spending so much time near the highway. These young bears were just following what mom taught and stayed where they felt most secure. The two yearlings were still together and remained highly visible until they were successfully relocated to a remote location in early July.

In the fall, two hunters from Wisconsin were strapped into a homemade harness that they used to drag along a freshly killed deer. Something was tugging on the carcass; it turned out to be this same radio-collared female grizzly. Food was scarce and she had followed her nose to a promising source. One man had bear spray, but it was not accessible. According to the hunters, the bear showed no aggression other than trying to steal the meat, but they decided to shoot her. They were strapped in, probably couldn't maneuver out of the harness quickly, and were not taking any chances at such close range. Had bear spray been used, it could have prevented the killing of this animal.

Habitat

Shoshone National Forest is prime grizzly bear habitat just to the east of Yellowstone Park. The dense woodland and dramatic peaks remind me of northwestern Montana. After coming out of their dens, bears search first for winter-killed and weakened animals because this area is such good ungulate winter range. Predation of moose calves has been observed near the North Fork of the Shoshone River, and elk are abundant. I suspect that many elk calves fall prey to bears here, but these events are seldom seen.

As in neighboring Yellowstone Park, meat constitutes a high percentage of the diets of these bears, but a distinctive feature of this area is the early spring green-up. Annual bear densities here vary but, in years when food has been scarce in much of the surrounding area, many bears have been seen chowing down in the lush pockets of Shoshone vegetation and appear to have taken full advantage of this short-lived resource. The preferred vegetation includes grasses, biscuitroot, dandelions, cow parsnip, and clover. By mid-June in most years, grizzlies leave the area to begin following the green-up to higher elevations, feeding mostly on roots, tubers, and corms. They then seek out army cutworm moth sites and whitebark pine nuts. In the fall or earlier in a poor year for moths or pine nuts, the great bear often roams lower elevations seeking vegetation along river bottoms.

The scene was dramatically different in the spring of 2001, with bear sightings less frequent. After an extremely mild winter, unseasonably early spring green-up seemed to be a possibility. But with so little moisture in the ground, the forage was never good. Some bears arrived early because of the warm weather but found little to munch on. When cool wet weather moved back in, most bears left to check out other places or

▲ *Clover*

▲ *Biscuitroot*

simply laid low, waiting for conditions to change.

At times it must be difficult for bears to decide how much energy to expend in search of food. Many bears lose weight during the spring and early summer as they continue to live off winter fat reserves, but their dietary requirements are not as intense this time of year as they will be

▲ *Elk thistle*

▲ *Cow parsnip*

later in the season. A bear may be subjected to additional weight loss if it travels widely without obtaining much nutrition. Those that do may be at a disadvantage because bigger bears usually dominate the prime feeding spots.

Another factor contributing to the scarcity of bears that spring may have been the large number of human-caused mortalities that occurred here in the previous year. And after such an easy winter for ungulates, it is likely that winter-killed carrion was scarce. This all serves to illustrate how drastically conditions can change from year to year.

▲ *Dandelion*

Different Attitude

This cautious mother bear cruised the forest with her two yearling cubs. On three occasions I watched her bluff-charge cars and people on the road, once from clear across the river. This bear family foraged the same area, during the same year, as the mother bear who was killed by the Wisconsin hunters. The cubs of the two families were the same age. But these three bears were considerably larger, and this mother bear had an entirely different demeanor.

The two families were subjected to similar environmental and human-related factors, but this big mother seemed older and more experienced. She preferred to stay away from people. These three wary bruins often surveyed a portion of their home range early in the morning but didn't stick around. I rarely saw them feed close to the road. All three were together when I last spotted them on a distant hillside in early June.

Autumn Foods

T he young grizzly emerged into the early morning sunlight, patrolling the riverbank. It was late September and brilliant yellow foliage was just beginning to illuminate the countryside. He quickly found a dense thicket of rose bushes and began voraciously plucking off the bright red rose hips from the prickly, branched stems. The hungry bear spent over an hour inhaling the vitamin-rich fruits from this large bunch before moving on. Rose bushes were plentiful, and the bruin often gobbled up scores of rose hips without much effort.

During his daily travels, the same young bear consumed black chokecherries. When they ripened in late summer, these tart cherries had a sparkling red color and were far more plentiful. Now, the small round fruits had turned black in their final seasonal stage. Although still favored by the bears, chokecherries had become a secondary food source, no longer abundant and probably less nutritious this time of year. When this bear did find a decent patch, he often stood on his hind legs while pulling the slender shrubs to the ground with his front paws. He then pinned them down and easily fed on the black cherries, looking rather like a dog chewing on a bone. Other times he pushed a thick branch down to his level, then braced his front paws against it while plucking every reachable berry with his mouth. After a long feeding session, the scene often looked like a herd of bison had just trudged through, with green leaves and long stems matted close to the ground.

Throughout this critical time of year, the days were getting shorter and this grizzly was continuously active. I often observed him several hours a day as he walked many miles up and down the river. The preferred source of nutrition was obviously the rose hips and chokecherries; he revisited the same

patches repeatedly. Between berries, he dug up roots and munched on clover and grasses along his travel route.

During hot Indian summer days, he usually took a mid-afternoon break to soak in the river. The young bruin submerged only part of his body, including all four legs and belly, but was able to stay in one spot by delicately paddling upstream at just the right pace. The river ran low this time of year and the current was relatively mild. He showed great strength and buoyancy, with paws surging forward through the clear water while his upper body appeared still. This bear looked refreshed and energetic when he stepped out of the river, water dripping off his shiny coat. He had strategically positioned himself close to a prime berry patch, and it was time to eat.

The small grizzly remained along the river corridor because most of the surrounding countryside was dry, with little nutrition to be found. It is possible that his mother had followed the same routes, making this familiar territory.

Grizzlies around here are not always so visible this time of year. They strongly prefer to be eating whitebark pine nuts at remote high elevations. The whitebarks had, however, failed this year, and bears were forced to wander far and wide seeking alternative foods.

Some bears chose this area even though they were subjected to human disturbance along the road. Others found their calories in isolated wilderness, far away from any civilization. Some hung around hunting camps looking for gut piles and scraps.

A Shady Afternoon Siesta

y mid-October, the grizzlies I observed were primarily digging up and consuming roots. Often a bear would move its butt around in a circular fashion while digging in one spot for a couple of hours, never moving more than twenty feet in any direction. Clover and clover roots were ingested along with various grasses. The chokecherries were now shriveled up and no longer an option. Bears often walked through the same dense clusters of rose bushes that they had gorged on just a couple of weeks ago. Although rose hips were still abundant, the bruins showed little interest. These firm fruits are available up until hibernation and remain on the vine all winter.

Late Grizzlies

C old, snowy weather was set-tling in during late October as two sub-adult grizzlies lin-gered in the area. They continued dig-ging and eating grasses while ignoring available rose hips. It is vital that these young bears put on as much weight as possible before winter. At the same time, bears can reach the point of diminishing returns in their continuing search for food. It is easy for a bear to use up more calories searching than it is able to take in. If bears stay extremely active in these conditions without eating much, they can actually lose weight and enter their dens without adequate fat reserves. In some cases, the energy they conserve now may be the difference between life and death.

As temperatures continued to drop and the ground froze, both grizzlies disappeared—I hope because they knew when to quit even though winter had come early. I did not see either bear again after October 26, though later that week I did see fresh tracks of two different adult grizzlies.

A mysterious bear seemed to be constantly foraging in the shadows. Although he was close to the road, the dark male remained secretive, keeping thick trees and bushes between him and human observers. Twice I saw tourists try to approach a little closer for a good picture, and both times he warned them by making a short threatening bluff charge, then immediately returning to feed as the would–be photographers scurried back to their respective cars.

After watching him a while for the first time, I noticed something unusual about his nose. At first I thought some wet vegetation was clinging to it, or it could have been a scar. I observed him for several hours and, although he never came into full view, the nose just did not look normal. But he obviously was not going to make it easy for me by emerging into the bright sunlight.

Shortly after the sun dipped below the horizon, he walked out into a nearby open meadow. I grabbed my spotting scope for a close–up look and saw a huge, deep laceration on his nose with little pieces hanging down. This may have been the result of an altercation with another bear. The wound was severe enough to affect his nasal passages. I had seen many a battle–scarred male grizzly before, but nothing like this.

For three days, he followed the same pattern of meandering on the edge of civilization but making a full appearance only after the sun went down. I wanted to get a picture of the nose, but he continued to maintain a veil of secrecy. Except for this wound, he seemed to be in excellent physical shape, and I guessed his age to be five or six years. Each night I left him foraging in the dark.

On the morning of October 28, fresh snow covered the landscape and the temperature had dipped into single digits. The ground was very hard. To my surprise, the wounded bear was eating vegetation right next to the road. After

previously being so shy, he now did not appear to be concerned about the four automobiles that stopped nearby. Fortunately, everyone stayed in their vehicles, and I was able to take pictures from the window of my van. After less than twenty minutes out in the open, he calmly turned away and walked slowly but deliberately uphill to the north and quickly disappeared into the thick forest. The early wintry weather had settled in, and he may have headed toward a den site. With the sub–adults apparently long gone, this wary bear with the lacerated nose was the last grizzly I saw in Shoshone National Forest that year.

Glacier National Park

After two solid weeks of rain, the skies were clearing as I gazed at an unbelievable rainbow from the foot of Bowman Lake. The brilliant colors, flanked by a vast panorama of peaks and lush verdant forest dotted with golden western larch, appeared to have dropped straight down from the heavens right into the middle of the lake. This was by far the widest and brightest rainbow I had ever seen. It lasted close to half an hour before the colors gradually faded into the distant landscape. Unfortunately, I had no camera with me at the time, but the image is indelibly etched into my memory. This was my first day ever in Glacier and the first day of Indian summer, 1973.

Ever since that remarkable late September day, I've had an ongoing love affair with this breathtaking country. Unlike Yellowstone, Glacier has a

◀ *Wary bear, early evening*

▲ *St. Mary Lake*

▲ *Lake Josephine*

limited road system and is primarily a hikers' park. With phenomenal trails and vast unspoiled acreage away from established routes, the potential for exploring is unlimited. Having covered thousands of miles in this remote rugged terrain, I've barely scratched the surface. Each new area is seemingly more dramatic than the last. Glacier National Park is the centerpiece of the Northern Continental Divide Ecosystem and possibly the wildest area remaining south of Canada.

▲ *Bowman Lake*

Habitat

Glacier's grizzlies must rely primarily on a vegetarian diet and are not nearly as large as the more carnivorous coastal bears of Alaska. The grizzlies here are comparable in size to other interior populations, like those found in Yellowstone and Denali national parks. Plant life is lush and diversified, both in lower-elevation coniferous forests and on the alpine tundra above timberline. An observant hiker will notice a potpourri of bear foods throughout the scenic backcountry.

In the spring and early summer, grizzlies travel the countryside consuming succulent vegetation such as horsetail, cow parsnip, grasses, and glacier lily flowers in avalanche chutes and at low elevations. They also dig up roots, eat overwintered bearberries (kinnikinnick), excavate ground squirrels, and feast on any carrion that can be found. Many grizzlies follow the green-up to higher elevations after the snow melts. As in the Yellowstone ecosystem, army cutworm moths found on remote talus slopes are an important but inconsistent grizzly bear food.

Later in the fall when fruity berries are no longer available, grizzlies settle for less nutritious mountain ash and bearberries. In addition, they often till massive areas to extract glacier lily and spring beauty corms (bulbs) prior to the long winter sleep. Columbian ground squirrels are early hibernators and often become easy prey. As the squirrels sleep helplessly in their dens, the grizzlies dig them up and chow down.

Bears are individuals, and each has its own familiar territories and preferences. These mountain grizzlies have no reliable source of nourishment like salmon, so "all established patterns" are subject to change, and food-dependent seasonal travel can vary dramatically from one year to the next.

▲ *Beargrass*

▼ *Glacier lilies, Flattop Mountain*

▼ *Mountain ash*

Avalanche Effects

It was early May, the skies were clearing, and I was walking the pavement at 6:30 A.M. Lower portions of Going-To-The-Sun road are usually accessible to hikers and bikers this time of year before opening to motorized vehicles. Shiny white mountain goats grazed peacefully on steep, hanging meadows high above. A mile east of Avalanche Creek, I glanced up at a nearby avalanche chute. A big grizzly was feeding on a mountain goat carcass less than one hundred yards away in the crusty snow. As I stopped and stood motionless, the bear lifted his head and stared directly at me for a few seconds and then resumed feeding. He had a large drooping belly and looked to be in great shape. After more gorging, the big guy tore a huge piece of meat off the carcass and slowly carried it into the thick bushes nearby as he glanced back toward me. The observation lasted twelve minutes. I found a distant vantage point and watched the spot all day but never saw the bear again that day as numerous unsuspecting bikers and hikers passed by.

The next morning I was out early again and, knowing the situation, stayed far away and went directly to my lookout so as not to disturb the bear for a second time. The burly bruin was resting on the snow near the carcass, and this time I was able to watch him for over an hour until two talkative men came along. The male grizzly immediately darted into nearby alders as the oblivious hikers walked by. As he followed a path high above the road, I watched him continue far to the south, mostly through the timber, as he headed toward Avalanche Creek.

The grizzly was long gone when I checked out the site a few hours later with my friend Art Sedlack, a former Glacier National Park ranger. When we examined the carcass, it was obvious that the female goat had been buried and frozen, probably by an avalanche, and the bear had been digging it out. One side of the goat's face and hindquarters had been skinned by a long fall. The legs were frozen deep into the snow and the goat lay in an icy grave, which probably prevented the bear from dragging it to cover. By counting the rings on the horns, Art estimated the nanny to be seven to nine years old. Bear tracks and scat surrounded the scene. Winter-killed ungulates are an important spring food source for bears around here, but carrion had likely been scarce during recent mild winters. The big grizzly was feeding mostly at night and relishing his early prize.

In similar circumstances, I once observed a young male foraging on lush vegetation just below an avalanche chute on a high, north-facing slope. I could barely see movement through the trees until he began to ascend on the open

snowfield. He crossed directly through an area where, judging by snow paths heading all the way down the steep slope, recent avalanches had occurred. It looked like skiers had beaten down the trail. The grizzly stepped off the snow and rested briefly on a narrow ledge before disappearing into the forest. Moments later mounds of snow came thundering down right where the bear had just been. It was a close call and I wondered if he sensed the impending danger—and then I wondered how many bears get buried by sudden avalanches while checking out chutes during the early spring green-up.

Sharing the Park Trails

On a spring day when sections of Going-To-The-Sun Road were plowed but had not yet been opened to cars, Tim Rubbert and I were walking the pavement in the early morning. By late afternoon we were still without a bear sighting, even though we had hiked many miles and just about worn out our binoculars "glassing" the high snowy avalanche chutes. It had been a long frustrating day as we sat down at a prime viewing location and both fell asleep.

After a short snooze, we were abruptly awakened by the sound of an urgent female voice. A woman riding a bicycle slowed down to say, "There's a big grizzly coming right down the road behind me," and then she sped off. We stood right up but, being a bit groggy, we didn't think quickly enough to ask many questions. Also, based on our experience over the years, we had learned that so many of these reports turn out to be wrong. Besides, if there was a bear walking on the road, how did the cyclist get past it?

We will never know but, in a few moments, sure enough a small grizzly was sauntering in our direction. The bear paused when it saw us, then came a little closer as we stood motionless. There was nowhere for us to go without thrashing through the brush, so we maintained our position. The wary young bear turned submissively sideways and carefully entered the woods. Although no longer visible, we could hear the bruin breaking brush as it circled around through the thick cover. We heard no vocalizations but

a lot of twigs were snapping. The bear had Tim and me in full view as it cautiously stepped back onto the pavement on the other side of us. The head swayed a little but there was no sign of aggression as the bruin turned away and strolled down the road. This bear was taking our only way out, so we allowed plenty of time before heading back along the same route.

The Grizzly That Couldn't Hide

On another early spring hike along Going-To-The Sun Road, I heard thrashing through dense cover. I turned and immediately saw this grizzly watching me. The leaves in the underbrush had not yet sprouted, so the bear seemed naked, "hiding" in cover that was not there. We looked at each other for a moment, then both cautiously exited in opposite directions. It's obviously easier to spot animals in these areas before the landscape greens up. A few weeks later, I may not have seen this bear.

On a sunny spring day over twenty years ago, I was hiking alone to Red Eagle Lake on the east side of the park, about fifteen miles roundtrip. The endeavor provided a little extra challenge this time of year because the two seasonal footbridges had not yet been erected for the summer hiking season and the raging creek was not safe to ford. Under the circumstances, I was forced to bushwhack through a lot of dense vegetation to reconnect with the trail four separate times.

Three huge bull elk, with velvet antlers shimmering in the bright light, grazed in a small meadow close to the trail. Near the lake, two bighorn rams nervously crossed in front of me. Bighorns are generally most secure in steep environments and feel much more vulnerable in this relatively flat, low-elevation terrain. Upon seeing me, the pair of rams changed gears from a lope to a gallop and headed directly toward some nearby rocky cliffs.

After a hearty lunch on a bluff above Red Eagle Lake, I began the return route. About halfway back as I rounded a blind corner, my brisk hiking pace came to an abrupt halt. A light brown grizzly was perched right on the trail about forty

yards away, staring in my direction with its head down. Just after our eyes met, I slowly sidestepped about ten feet off the trail and positioned myself purposefully behind a big tree trunk. Without warning, the bear ran straight down the trail toward me. I was relatively inexperienced at the time and wasn't sure what to do. I did not carry bear spray back then, and running certainly was not an option. I instinctively stood my ground behind the tree. When the grizzly got close, I yelled at the top of my lungs, "Go on!" The bear never broke stride as it passed very close by on the trail and then veered off into the woods. I listened to the fading sound of crashing in the underbrush as the startled bruin continued lumbering away through the dense forest.

I breathed a huge sigh of relief. The bear had made no vocalizations and I don't know if this was a "charge," but he was never headed directly toward me. Without the bridges, I was sure that no humans had been on the trail yet this year, and my presence may have obstructed the bear's preferred travel route. With few hikers around, bears generally use the trails more in spring and fall.

Another of my early experiences in Glacier Park was on an autumn day while hiking alone on a remote old trail near Logging Lake. This area seemed completely wild; the trail had not been maintained in many years. It was a densely forested area and, for some reason, I had an eerie feeling walking through this dark canyon of trees.

A while later, fresh shallow bear diggings began to appear on the edges of the trail and were becoming more frequent. Then I came upon a major warning sign: two large, fresh bear scats carefully positioned close together right in the middle of the trail, both still steaming.

A chill ran up my spine. I had a strong feeling that a grizzly bear was telling me the trail was not big enough for the both of us. I am stubborn and determined, but this was one time I turned around on a hike. In this kind of country with limited visibility, a surprise close encounter is much more likely than out in the open.

While hiking the Swiftcurrent Trail in the Many Glacier area on a warm summer day back in 1986, I spotted a female grizzly with two spring cubs foraging about one hundred yards from the trail. A few other hikers stopped and watched the bears with me. The mother was fully aware of our presence. She looked up at us a few times but seemed calm and unconcerned.

Suddenly she huffed and glared intently in our direction, and the cubs gathered close behind her. I had no idea what had suddenly changed her demeanor until I turned around and saw one of the hikers running away. This obviously got the bear's attention and caused her sudden mood change. Fortunately, she did not charge. The rest of us stood our ground and then slowly left the area.

Two Medicine Family

This grizzly bear family crossed the trail about twenty yards in front of me near Two Medicine Lake in the southeast corner of the park. The bears stopped a short distance away to check me out but showed no aggression as I calmly stood my ground. They then turned and walked steadily up the mountain, continuing in the same direction they were headed when I first saw them.

Grizzly Scratches
on Bridge

This bear sloshed through Swiftcurrent Creek and stopped on the far side of the small bridge near the Swiftcurrent trailhead. For a few minutes, the bruin scratched and rubbed on the bridge and surrounding rocks before heading toward Fishercap Lake. I hiked over to the lake and watched the grizzly take a playful bath in the early morning sunlight.

On a clear early morning in late July, Tim Rubbert and I watched a lone grizzly peacefully eating huckleberries high above the Iceberg Lake trail. Another grizzly approached from below and crossed the trail in front of us, heading toward the other bear. Approaching slowly at first, the second bear broke into a dead run and chased the first bear across the hillside above, then down to the trail about seventy-five yards from our position.

The bears were scuffling on the trail with dirt flying everywhere when two female hikers came around a blind corner. From what we saw, the sparring bears paid no attention to the shocked girls, who nonetheless exited abruptly. After the brief skirmish, the aggressor walked a few yards in our direction and then up the hill, claiming the best huckleberry patch. The loser laid on the trail for a few minutes before slowly moving downhill.

Other hikers came along and took pictures. This bear stopped to eat a few huckleberries along the way before vanishing into the thick brush far below the trail. Neither bear appeared injured, but the winner successfully asserted its dominance.

This grizzly was eating huckle-berries near a heavily used trail, going about his business and seeming to be unconcerned about all the hikers who gathered to watch. But when the bear made a short bluff charge and started to move down toward the trail, the people backed off. The adult male grizzly came onto the trail and, with flared nostrils, briefly faced the group of humans. Then, with no further sign of aggression, he slowly turned and walked below the trail, calmly resuming feeding as if nothing had happened. Many hikers passed by along the trail after that, and the bear stayed close for a while before gradually moving away. I think the grizzly let us know that we were blocking his path and, having successfully crossed the trail, he was no longer agitated.

Off the Trail, Alert and Wary

Tim Rubbert was about twenty yards ahead of me as we walked a remote ridgetop on the west side of the park. On one of the downhill sections of the long ridge, an agitated bull moose burst out of the timber snorting, then made an immediate detour back into the trees farther ahead. We thought the animal was reacting to us until a silver-tipped grizzly with a yearling cub appeared. She was huffing, close behind the moose and within fifteen yards of Tim. When the mother bear saw Tim, she popped her jaw nervously, turned, and scurried back into cover right behind her nervous cub. They were following the same exit path as the moose. I snapped this one picture of the mother bear just before she disappeared.

While I was sitting with Tim Rubbert at a distant observation point well above the trail, a big grizzly came down from the rolling slope across the way. He approached our scent and then slammed to a stop and spun away, galloping for parts unknown.

On another day we saw similar behavior in his same area. Her shoulders mantled in shining silver, a mother grizzly and her two spring cubs approached rapidly. They had not detected us, so we carefully moved away and climbed up the nearby bluffs. From this safe vantage point, we watched the three bears come to the very spot we had just left. The female immediately paused and rotated her powerful nose through the air as she sorted out the situation. After a few seconds, she swiveled and they stampeded away. This was a valuable lesson for the cubs, and I hope they don't forget it.

I believe these two instances to be typical grizzly bear reaction to any fresh human sign in this ecosystem, but such behavior is rarely observed. Although these bears never saw us, they were very cautious and reacted quickly to our scent. There was no hesitation. They definitely wanted to avoid humans.

Moths on Mount Cleveland

I took this picture of Tim Rubbert near the top of Stony Indian Peaks on our aborted attempt to climb Mount Cleveland, the highest peak in the park. Our goal was to observe grizzlies consuming army cut-worm moths on the mountain, but this is as far as we got because the remaining route looked too dangerous. From our base camp near Stony Indian Pass, it was a major challenge just to get to this point, and it took us much more time than we had anticipated. The traveling was slow as we climbed steadily in the early morning sunlight up across a long, rugged mountainside, trying to follow goat trails wherever possible. The footing was unstable and loose rocks were flying everywhere. We are strong hikers but not climbers. After talking it over, we were both obviously uncomfortable in this terrain and decided not continue on a precipitous ledge where one slip would result in a fifteen-hundred-foot fall straight down.

On the most distant high peak behind Tim in the picture, the very top of Mount Cleveland, we spotted three grizzlies eating moths. We could see them well thanks to the spotting scope and tripod we carried up the mountain. The sighting made this trip a success.

Huckleberries

During the best of times, when the landscape is moist and fertile, grizzlies can choose from a wide variety of berries including serviceberry, raspberry, soapberry, elder-berry, thimbleberry, grouse whortleberry, hawthorn berry, snowberry, devil's club berry, bearberry, and mountain ash. They eat them all at one time or another, but there's no berry like the huckleberry. It is one of the most nutritious bear foods in the ecosystem and highly pre-ferred when abundant. In this region, secluded ripe huckleberry patches are a bear's idea of pure heaven. They pluck off the "hucks" while stripping leaves and twigs. These meaty berries are the only natural non-meat source that I have seen to create extraordinarily high concentrations of grizzlies.

Sweet juicy huckleberries are a truly fabulous tasty treat. I'm salivating right now imagining deep purple huckleber-ries at my fingertips along the trail. For-tunately, I have some stashed in the freezer and, though far from being freshly picked, the taste is still great and they remind me of the huckleberry bears.

Elderberries

A good stand-by food source in Glacier, these purple elderberries are not much like the abundant, plump red elderberries loved by bears on Kodiak Island, Alaska.

Tim Rubbert and I stood on the ridgetop overlooking at least twenty-two grizzlies carefully picking their way through the rugged hillsides of an isolated mountain basin. We were witnessing a truly amazing spectacle as all these bears jockeyed for position near the choice berry patches while carefully trying to avoid each other. We observed a few minor confrontations but no serious conflicts among the bears. This was a bumper crop year and there were plenty of berries to go around. Family groups, individuals, and a pair of siblings seemingly came from miles around for "prime time" huckleberries.

In the heat of the day, a lone grizzly was creating an interesting mud trail across the lake below. The bear was prob-ably just cooling off before getting back to the huckleberries. We've returned to the area several times but never again seen anything like it; berry production in this location has declined in recent years.

In the summer of 1992, a good crop of huckleberries ripened early and the bears gorged. A big storm came through in late August, dumping over a foot of heavy wet snow on the high country. The next day Tim Rubbert and I trudged up to a familiar lookout above a remote valley just below the Continental Divide. Post-holing up a mountain through deep snow is never a picnic. We crossed several sets of fresh bear tracks on the route. Our efforts were rewarded because that afternoon we saw eight grizzlies and thirteen black bears eating huckleberries in the snow. The next day I went up alone and saw nine grizzlies and eight black bears. It was to be the last huckleberry feast of the year up here, and the bears knew it. With this big blast of early winter, the berries were rapidly softening and falling prematurely off the vine.

Four years later I journeyed to the same area on September 27. There had already been several small snowstorms at this elevation but no severe cold, and most of the snow had melted. To my astonishment, the huckleberries actually seemed to be improving at this late date, though I saw only two grizzlies. Tim and I came back up on September 30. These late huckleberries hit a short peak and were as sweet as I've ever tasted. We saw twelve grizzlies scattered around the valley. On the way down, a grizzly mother and two yearling cubs were foraging close to the trail. The cubs huddled nervously behind mom as she stopped and calmly watched us from a nearby huckleberry patch. We stood our ground until they retreated into the valley. It was much cooler when I returned alone the next day. I saw only one grizzly and a lot of mushy berries. Conditions had changed quickly again.

Serviceberries

I n recent years throughout the Glacier ecosystem, huckleberries have not been the dependable mainstay they once were. Some years have been spotty and others complete failures. One hot summer when the huckleberries ripened about a month early at mid-elevations on the east side of Glacier National Park, they were burned out and mushy before the third week of August, and the bears I observed immediately switched over to serviceberries.

In many areas I have studied year after year, serviceberries seem to be the clear second choice. These berries have a color similar to huckleberries but are less juicy and coarser in texture. In some years when there have been few huckleberries available on the east side, grizzlies foraged heavily on abundant serviceberry crops.

A Summer Crossing

Grizzlies are often seen in Bear Valley from Granite Park Chalet. They are usually far away and best viewed through a spotting scope. When I worked at the chalet in the summers of 1996 and 1997, rarely did a day go by when I didn't see at least one grizzly in the area. September 1, 1997, would have been my mother's seventieth birthday. I was inside the chalet that day when someone said that there were "four or five grizzlies near the trail" to the north. Four great hiking trails funnel into Granite Park, and bears use them most often late in the season when there is decreased human activity.

I walked up a hillside behind the chalet to get a good look. I didn't see anything at first, but I heard the unmistakable sound of cubs bawling. About ten minutes passed before a mother grizzly with two spring cubs emerged from the trees and began digging just below the trail that comes down from Ahern Pass. I spotted two hikers coming and was ready to yell to them if the bears did not move on. The bear family did move on and continued traveling steadily uphill. I could see that they were headed straight for the heavily used portion of the trail that traverses Swiftcurrent Pass. The hikers I was concerned about came through and never saw the bears. I then scrambled uphill across a big switchback

toward the Swiftcurrent Trail to relocate the bears.

The bears were ambling near the trail as a man hid behind a large boulder just a few feet away trying to take pictures. When the bears moved on, I asked the man if he would feel safer walking with me. He said yes and joined me without his backpack. I told him that he could not leave his pack on the trail and, after some mild resistance, he went back to retrieve it.

As the three bears approached the pass, they angled their way onto the trail as two unsuspecting hikers were approaching. I yelled over the bears to the hikers and fortunately they were able to understand me. Following my instructions, they moved well above the trail and allowed the bears to pass by without incident. They joined me as we followed the bears over the pass at a safe distance. I had previously seen this bear family a few times in the Many Glacier area, and the female had never been aggressive toward people. All the same, any bear can be dangerous if put in a difficult situation, especially a mother with cubs. They probably came up here looking for huckleberries. The bears crossed three snowfields. Mom walked purposefully, but the cubs just wanted to play. They wrestled on the snowfields, snow flying through the air each time one of the cubs pivoted to face the other. A couple of times, they tumbled over and over together on the crusty snow, nipping at each other's ears. All three swam in a small pond at the bottom of the third snowfield to cool off, then rejoined the trail. In much drier conditions a couple of years later, there were no snowfields and the pond was bone dry in late summer.

The three bears walked on but quickly disappeared into a covered part of the trail. We yelled ahead to hikers coming up from the other side. It took three determined voices, but they finally understood us and turned around. I was sure the bears had bedded down on or near the trail, since we had looked everywhere but did not see them emerge. Other hikers came up from behind and were reluctant to believe that grizzlies might be blocking the trail. I escorted six hikers across rocky terrain,

making a wide circle around the portion of the trail where the bear family was last seen, then down to a lower part of the trail where they walked out. I never did see those bears again and will never know what might have happened. The one thing I do know is that all the bears and humans involved in this experience made it safely through the day.

Scrawny Bears

Since 1999, Tim Rubbert and I have seen far fewer grizzlies in traditional berry "hot spots" and throughout the park. We've also seen more thin, apparently undernourished grizzlies like this one than ever before, and very few family groups. During this period, bears traveled extensively in search of calories and visited places where they hadn't been seen for a long time. Although grizzlies have moved primarily into former habitat, some of these "new" areas are now inhabited by private land owners and small communities. Many folks believe that, because grizzlies are expanding their current ranges, the bear population is increasing. This might not be the case. It may be that the bruins are starving up in the mountains and have been forced to come down. This could, then, be a sign of fewer rather than more bears. Remember, grizzly bear survival depends primarily on the quality of the habitat.

We know that bears must adapt constantly to the changing environment. From our observations, they have been less concentrated in recent years. But if drought conditions persist, this core area may not be able to support historic numbers of grizzlies. Although Tim and I frequent many remote backcountry locations annually, we cannot discount the fact that the great bear may have been finding food in other isolated sites where they are not easily observable. It's impossible for us to be everywhere. Sadly, because more grizzlies have wandered close to civilization, human-caused mortality has increased significantly for the bears. Tim and I are not formal scientists, but we are dedicated to our studies and put in an enormous amount of "field time" with our subjects. We do not like the current trend in our firsthand observations. There are strong signs that dry weather and poor berry production are adversely affecting the grizzlies of Glacier.

The Dry Summer of 2003

From the foot of Lake McDonald, I watched in amazement as the Trapper Fire plumed high above the famous Garden Wall to the north. Looking west, I noticed another fire billowing into the clear blue sky behind Apgar Lookout. The scene had been calm and peaceful when my wife Ingrid, my dog Merle, and I were in that vicinity just a couple hours earlier, swimming in the Flathead River. This was July 23 at about 6:00 P.M., and this new blaze was named the Robert Fire. It would eventually consume more than 57,000 acres. Daily temperatures reached into the mid-90s, there had been no measurable rain in a while, and this was the sixth consecutive summer of drought in the region. The fires began in mid-July, about a month early for fire season around here even in a bad year. New fires were popping up often, and there wasn't enough manpower to fight them all. The blazes were spreading rapidly and did not subside until cool weather moved in and heavy rains soaked the landscape in September. All told, the fires in the Glacier area consumed more than 170,000 acres, mostly in the park. Fires burned more than 650,000 acres within the state of Montana.

Prime grizzly bear habitat was burning, and I wondered where the bears would go in this changing environment. During these past few extremely dry years, bears had already seemed scarce. What effect would these massive fires have on Glacier's grizzlies? Much of the area would regenerate itself, but this natural process would take many years.

The scenic Iceberg Lake Trail had been closed for two weeks, first because of fire danger and then, the last few days, because a grizzly bear family was frequenting the area. This is a popular travel route used extensively by both day hikers and backpackers. The trail reopened on the afternoon of August 4.

On the cool, clear morning of August 5, my sister Tootsie and I were at a lookout point near the trail when we spotted the mother grizzly and her two spring cubs eating serviceberries on a steep slope high above. We pointed out the bruins to bear ranger Bob Adams, who was out early to monitor the situation. The bear family was foraging in a very dry area, and we all knew that at some point they would have to come down and cross the trail to find water. Bob was concerned that they might linger on or near the trail. The bears soon traveled high to the west, then dropped down into the heavy cover just below tree line. They were not seen for a while, so Bob left to patrol a different area.

The vegetation around the Iceberg Trail was the driest I had ever seen it this time of year. Leaves were already turning brown and berries were sparse. Huckleberries, serviceberries, soapberries, and elderberries were all available, but nothing was abundant. With the forage so poor, I wondered what was keeping bears in this valley. Maybe they just couldn't find a place with better food sources, maybe they felt secure in this location. Nevertheless, all the bruins around here were having to work hard for their meals.

Later that morning the grizzly bear family reappeared out in the open about two hundred yards above the trail. Bob had just returned because a single grizzly was reported to be near this trail, but he never saw such a bear and neither did we. Meanwhile, as the hot sun baked the area for yet another unrelenting day, the bear family slowly began moving down toward the trail, stopping often to munch on serviceberries. As the bears got closer, Bob began to warn passing hikers that the trail could close again today. He certainly did not want to close this trail again. After all, it had been reopened for less than twenty-four hours, and another closure would affect many people. First and foremost, though, Bob had to consider the safety of bears and humans and do everything possible to keep them apart.

The grizzly bear trio continued their downward movement along a vertical line of trees that formed the eastern boundary of the dry, open slope. Several hikers gathered to watch from below, and Bob yelled for them to get back. Although she showed no noticeable aggression, the mother bear did look a bit agitated as she approached to within fifty yards of the trail with her cubs in tow. Hikers were gathering to observe this spectacle, and some may have been blocking the mother bear's intended path across the trail. Bob became more emphatic and anxious but remained patient while trying to manage this growing situation. He continued to holler at the onlookers to move away, but most of the people did not respond. I don't know if they were ignoring him or just couldn't hear.

Bob's face displayed genuine concern as he observed the scene. Earlier, he had told Tootsie and I that this bear family was partially habituated and had been known to forage near the trail while appearing to ignore hikers. Because the trail is relatively easy, it gets used by people of all ages, including fathers carrying babies in seated backpacks and exuberant children who sometimes walk or run well ahead of their parents. Everyone is welcome on the trail, but most park visitors know little about bear behavior. Bob Adams considered this situation a serious risk to the animals and

humans. With this huge responsibility squarely on his shoulders, the decision was clear. Maintaining his observation position, at about high noon Bob looked all around one more time, slowly turned toward Tootsie and I and said, "The trail is closed," and proceeded to call in the news on his park service radio.

Bob asked us to walk out immediately, but the bears were now moving more purposefully down toward the trail and were about to cut us off. The mother bear and one of her cubs seemed concerned. The alert cub stood as they nervously looked in our direction. We slowly walked backward toward Bob while trying to keep the bears in view. We did not see them when we hiked out with Bob about ten minutes later, and we didn't know if they had crossed the trail.

Park rangers now had the daunting task of clearing all day hikers off this trail system as well as contacting backcountry campers who had planned to hike out this way. According to standard park policy, a trail can reopen only after rangers have patrolled it a minimum of two consecutive days without seeing bear activity nearby. Bob and the bear management team at Many Glacier prefer a minimum of three clear patrol days on the Iceberg Trail. It ended up staying closed for almost two more weeks, leaving the bears to forage in peace for a while.

lthough the bear family was still frequenting the area, the trail reopened on the afternoon of August 17. The three bears were now cruising all over the countryside in their quest for calories. One day they traveled more than five miles to the north through the Ptarmigan Tunnel but soon returned to the familiar open slopes near the Iceberg Lake trailhead. It seemed like mom was running her cubs ragged. On the morning of August 19, they were right on the trail as I hiked up early in the morning. I watched them walk the trail for a few minutes and then move up toward potential berry patches.

The bears continued to come near the trail at random times each day and, although the rangers attempted to follow their activities, they just couldn't be there every time the bears appeared. Finally, the park service decided to radio-collar the mother bear so that they could better monitor her whereabouts. This was to be the first step in an extended program of aversive conditioning. For that purpose, the trail was closed again on the morning of August 21. I was told that the bears were found near the trail and the mother tranquilized. The cubs apparently waited anxiously nearby as their mom was fitted with a radio collar. She had looked thin and seemed to be in poor condition for

this time of year, with a weight estimated at 220–250 pounds. The capture went smoothly, and they released her and reopened the trail at noon the same day.

The next morning was clear but very smoky. Tim Rubbert and I were up there just in time to see these bears—the mother with her new radio collar—amble down an open slope and cross the trail to the west of us. The three bruins seemed curious and wary but certainly not frightened. They walked on or near the trail for a few minutes, then quickly disappeared into the thick underbrush below.

Over the next few days, rangers used the telemetry to help locate the bears. In the beginning, when the bruins approached the trail, Bob recalls hitting the mother bear with bean bags and rubber bullets twice in one instance and once on another day. When the bears came near the trail after that, rangers engaged in shouting and clapping with some degree of success. Specially trained Karelian bear dogs were also used daily.

The dogs' persistent barking forced the bruins to retreat toward cover.

These methods were teaching the bears to avoid humans, and the strategy seemed to be working. The bears quickly became very leery of the people and the trail. While foraging on some familiar slopes, they often gazed down anxiously at the gathering spectators. They began to take wide circular routes above and below the trail, then try to sneak across it when no one was looking. After all the aversive conditioning, they no longer seemed comfortable around the trail when people were on it. Now, whenever the bears came to the trail, they crossed hurriedly and traveled well away before serious foraging began.

I have mixed feelings about what happened with these bears. On one hand, the rangers were effective in preventing a conflict between bears and humans. More important, in the long run this experience could prove to be a great lesson for the cubs, if they survive, because they'll learn

to avoid people and probably be much better off for doing so. In the short term, however, this aversive conditioning was dangerous to the bear family. This small mother bear appeared to be very low in the critical body fat needed to get through the winter. With calories already hard to come by, her travel patterns were altered and she endured additional stress. It remains to be seen whether she had the skill and intelligence to overcome these additional obstacles and get herself and her cubs through the winter. Because she wears a radio collar, we should eventually know the fate of these bears.

I have seen few grizzly bear cubs the past several years in this ecosystem and, for that matter, relatively few grizzlies. The present long-term drought is making for especially difficult times for an already endangered species—and, as this event shows, also especially difficult times for park service staff who must try to strike a balance between the survival of wildlife and the enjoyment of the park visitors.

Grizzly Claims Poached Moose

For three days in early October 1995, I watched a female adult grizzly feed on a young bull moose carcass in the Whitefish Mountain Range, four miles west of Glacier Park. A hunter apparently shot the moose illegally, and the bear claimed it on a clear-cut hillside about fifty yards above the dirt road near Red Meadow. As word of this sighting got out, many people came to watch. Nonetheless, the bear remained with the carcass out in the open. She had decided that it was worth putting up with human disturbance to take advantage of this rare opportunity. This female couldn't possibly have dragged the large carcass away, although I'm sure she would have liked to.

Many folks came and went, but I spent the entire three days there. No other predators challenged her, and I never saw any scavenging birds. This is partly explained by the way she attended her prize. She spent most of her time sleeping on top of this dead moose. She would awaken, quickly unbury it, and then eat for a while. When the carcass was open and exposed, the smell was very strong. After each feeding, she always meticulously reburied it with fresh sod and forest debris. The bear would dig foliage, turning it into a round shape, then roll it on top of the carcass with her front paws shoveling backward. As time went on, she

had to move a little farther from the site to find fresh vegetation. Each time she completed this process, the smell would virtually disappear. Bears usually try to conceal the smell of a carcass in an effort to eliminate competition. A bigger bear could have easily displaced this female. She spent far more time covering up the moose than unburying it and feeding combined.

Concerned that someone would come along and shoot this grizzly, government agencies decided to move the carcass. They used cracker shells to scare the bear into the woods and a winch to pull the moose down the hill, then lifted it into a pickup truck and drove it to a different drainage safely away from any open road.

I waited in my truck late in the after-noon. Everyone else was gone. The bear returned and, with a bewildered look, sniffed and licked around the area before following the carcass trail down to the road. She paced back and forth near my vehicle and then returned to the previous carcass site. Confused, she dug around but found only a few mea-ger scraps. She repeated the process, then finally gave up and exited into the woods. The moose was only about half eaten when it disappeared, but there was nothing the frustrated grizzly could do about it unless she found the carcass in its new location.

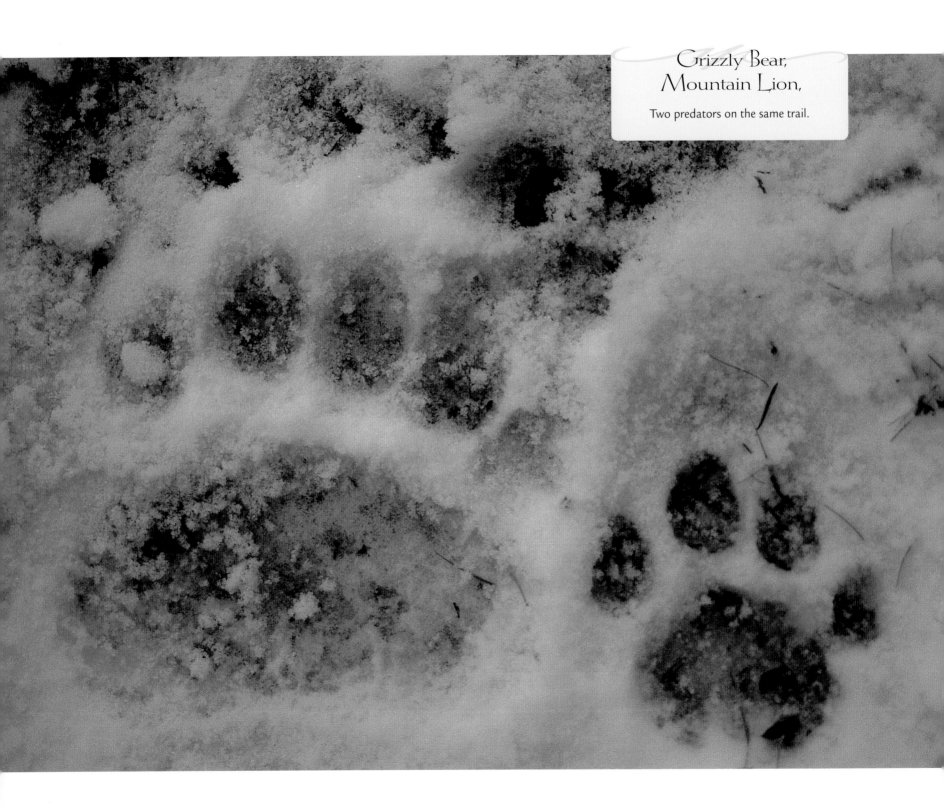

Grizzly Bear,
Mountain Lion,

Two predators on the same trail.

Signs of Winter Grizzlies

What a great time for tracking and hiking—an overcast day, about 29 degrees Fahrenheit, with about two inches of snow on the ground. In our bare feet, Tim Rubbert and I forded the middle fork of the Flathead River just east of Nyack Creek on December 3, 1997. Our chilly toes were just beginning to thaw out as we hiked toward Nyack Creek. When we crossed the fresh tracks of a large grizzly in the snow, we became exhilarated and immediately forgot that our feet were ever cold. Neither one of us had ever seen a grizzly bear in December. Unfortunately, the tracks led straight into thick cover with limited visibility.

As we walked around this area and back out to the river, a mature bald eagle landed on top of a nearby tree. We then began to see and hear ravens and magpies coming from all directions. They were concentrating at a spot seventy-five or so yards into the dark forest nearby, in the direction the bear tracks were headed. When we distinctly heard a branch snap in that area, we felt sure the grizzly was feeding on a carcass back there. We really wanted to see a December bear, but this was obviously a dangerous situation. We reluctantly decided to leave the area.

Hiking toward Nyack Creek on the way out, we cut the fresh tracks of two sub-adult grizzlies traveling away from the carcass site. On the basis of the size and direction of all the tracks, we determined that these young bears had probably been feeding on the carcass first and were displaced by the larger, more dominant bear.

This was an exciting day and great for the bears who took advantage of this late-season feast. We were a bit frustrated because at least three grizzlies were nearby and we never got to see any of them. And we still had to ford back through frigid water at the end of the day. Cold feet again.

After a long absence, in the early 1980s wolves began a natural migration back into the west side of Glacier Park from Canada. This heavily forested country surrounds the north fork of the Flathead River and also supports a healthy population of mountain lions. In one part of this area where these two predators thrive, I have seen fresh grizzly tracks in every winter month. Just one or two bears have spent the winters sniffing out kills and then hijacking them from the lions and wolves. The size of these tracks suggests that the winter bears are males, and the name of the game in the bear kingdom is size and dominance. The bigger bruins usually claim the best food sources and mating rites. Bears hibernate mainly because there is nothing for them to eat in the snow-covered landscape, and they usually lose about 25 percent of their body weight in the den. Any bear that can stay out during winter months productively and lose less weight will gain on the competition.

My Closest Encounter

In the early morning of September 29, 1993, Tim Rubbert and I were standing at the Packer's Roost trailhead, ready to embark on one of our last major hikes into grizzly country for the season. Having no clue what was in store for us, we had picked a glorious Indian summer day without a cloud in the sky. With the brilliant fall colors beginning to fade, this was likely to be the last period of good weather before snow began to pile up in the high country. We planned to hike twenty-four miles round trip to Fifty Mountain and return the same day.

Because of recent grizzly activity, the Fifty Mountain campground was closed to camping but open for day use, and the trail was posted with a bear warning.

The great peaks of Glacier Park surrounded our travels through one of the most awesome places on earth. On the way in, we hiked up and over Flattop Mountain, then leveled off through a series of small secluded meadows before we cut up to Fifty Mountain. We saw very little bear sign in these first twelve miles. Further along the trail on a high spot above the campground, we ate lunch in the middle of a huge meadow that looked like it had been methodically attacked by an army of rototillers. The area was loaded with glacier lilies. In the summer, grizzlies clip off the bright yellow flowers with their mouths. But at this time of the year, they intensely dig up the nutritional bulbs (corms) with their long claws and strong shoulders. With all of this recent sign around us, we glassed the immense open landscape thoroughly but did not see a single bear.

It was around 3:00 P.M. on our ascent back up Flattop Mountain. On this partially open hillside mixed with subalpine firs, we hadn't seen any fresh bear sign on our morning pass through here. As Tim continued to glass the distant slopes all the way over to the Highline Trail, I walked on about ten yards ahead, all the while continuing a spirited discussion about football.

All of a sudden I heard a huffing sound. I immediately looked up and clearly saw the distinct face of a light-colored sub-adult grizzly bear barreling toward me from within five yards. Time stood still in a sequence that lasted just a few seconds. There was no time to think or fear, but I knew exactly what was happening and what to do. There weren't any escape options and no time to grab the bear spray from my belt. I started to turn away but the young bruin was on me in an instant. Tim later said that the bear took a few round-house swings as I was falling to the ground but kept missing like an amateurish prizefighter. The bear ripped open my scalp with its mouth, bit into my left wrist as I tried to cover my head, tore off my camera holster, then pinned me firmly to the ground with one paw on my back. I was trying not to move, but it all happened so fast.

Tim fired a quick, loud burst of bear spray in the bear's direction. The grizzly turned and exploded directly into the red mist as Tim unleashed the full force of his spray. Tim kept spraying as the bear charged to within five feet of him, then turned away and fled downhill. The can was almost empty, but he had enough to do the job. Bear spray is most effective at close range, and I'm sure the young grizzly got a snoot full.

The next thing I remember was hearing Tim ask frantically, "Jim, are you okay?" With blood streaming down my face, I stood up and looked toward him. At that moment I was not in pain and had no idea how badly I was hurt. Tim hurried over as I noticed the laceration on my hand. We quickly assessed the situation and figured it was a surprise encounter. The bear had moved in sometime after we passed through this morning and probably made a day bed in the small patch of fir trees right next to the trail. The most likely scenario is that the grizzly was startled from an afternoon nap at close range and reacted defensively. This late in the year, few people are walking these trails, so it is common for bears to use them more frequently than in the summer. The trail system provides bears with easy travel routes.

We moved about thirty yards up the trail from the attack site, and I emptied the contents of my first aid kit onto the ground. At first Tim was concerned that the bear might return, but I figured this was as traumatic an experience for the young bruin as it was for me, and he'd be long gone by now. I felt no pain as Tim poured hydrogen peroxide over the open gash on my head. He wrapped my wrist with gauze and tape, then he

created a small bloody turban by covering my head with an Ace bandage, gauze, and a torn T-shirt. By the time we packed up and Tim took a few pictures to document the scene, it was close to 3:30. Tim put the heaviest items into his pack, including my camera gear.

All things considered, it could have been worse. I was focused and determined to pound my way home. Both of us knew exactly where we were, ten and a half miles from the car. Spending the night out there bleeding was not an option if I could help it.

With a lightened load I began climbing back up Flattop Mountain. Tim stayed behind to get organized. I hiked uphill with a flurry. There was a bounce to my step and I had a great rhythm going. I was thinking clearly but had no way of knowing how much was left in the tank and no realistic idea of how far I could get. Whenever I reached back to wipe the sweat from the back of my neck, my hand came away dripping with blood.

Tim caught up with me and, after about three miles, my pace had slowed considerably. I was beginning to weaken and could no longer carry any extra weight. With heavy packs, we were both well prepared for backcountry emergencies, which would be tested if we did not make it out that night. Tim nearly doubled his load when he tied my pack to

his as I again forged ahead.

My mind wandered along the trail as I fought for every mile. I knew that Tim and I were tomorrow's headlines and would have to deal with the media. Of course, this was assuming that we made it out tonight.

I ran out of gas with about four miles to go. We were in the dark forest now, with thick underbrush, and there was no place nearby for a rescue helicopter to land. We considered whether Tim should leave me and go for help. As we were mulling the options, an amazing revelation hit both of us at just about the same time. With all the excitement, neither one of us had anything to eat or drink since lunch more than five hours earlier. We immediately broke out the food, and I inhaled some protein bars and a lot of water. This made a world of difference. With renewed energy we headed down the mountain toward Mineral Creek.

The footbridge was out for the season but the water was shallow and easy to cross. Tim stood by as I sat down to take off my boots to ford the creek. With the safety clip gone, Tim inadvertently leaned on his bear spray, which was aimed directly at me. I was a sitting duck as the spray shot weakly toward my face. Fortunately, the can was almost empty and, after all, this was no big deal after what had just happened. We actually had a

good laugh. Today was not the only time Tim has accidentally sprayed me, and he has also nailed himself a few times.

The water was cold and new adrenaline had started to kick in. Except for one short uphill stretch, the last couple of miles were relatively easy. After battling for over four hours, to put it mildly, it was a major relief to see the car. With the shortened days, it was almost dark.

Tim sped to West Glacier, where we stopped to call Kalispell Regional Hospital. Coincidentally, a doctor was using an adjoining pay phone. He quickly checked me out and said I was doing fine. Monitored by police along the route, we raced down Highway 2 to the hospital, where a local television reporter was waiting with camera at the emergency room entrance. I would not allow photographs at that time and told Tim to get the person away. If the public saw me in this bloody state, the vivid visual picture would create additional fears and negative feelings about grizzly bears. After I was safely inside, Tim gave an interview.

My injuries were not overly severe. My hand was broken and had to be bandaged for the time being, and my head was stapled back together. Predictably, Tim and I were on the front pages of all the local newspapers for several days as more important news took a back seat. My friend Art Sedlack even read about the attack in *USA Today* while working in Uruguay. However, I wasn't dead, and no doctor said that I had a limited number of days left to live. Park service rangers investigated the scene and decided not to pursue the bear because the incident appeared to be a "defensive attack." We were familiar with park policy and expected this decision.

My broken hand was in a cast for twelve weeks and the overall recovery took longer than expected. I had naively thought that I would be back out hiking within a few weeks. One afternoon I stalked a brilliant red cardinal that was perched near the bird feeder in my sister's Chicago backyard. I always wanted to take a great picture of a red cardinal. When I took my camera with the telephoto lens out of the holster for the first time since the mauling, I discovered that the mirror in the viewfinder was cracked, and when I looked at the camera body I found a big canine tooth mark deep into the frame. At that moment I realized that the grizzly had actually bitten into my side, not just torn off my holster. Had it not been for the "protective" camera, I would probably have been more severely injured and unable to make the hike out.

To this day both Tim and I are comfortable hiking alone in grizzly country. We are cautious and understand the risks. The only change we've made is that each of us now carries two cans of bear spray. My parents taught me that, when you fall off a horse, it's best to get back on as soon as you can. I could hardly wait to get out into the back-country again but, realistically, I would have to wait patiently until spring.

Rocky Mountain Front

C learly defined prints in the dry mud along Blubber Creek exposed the travels of a grizzly. Much of the surrounding countryside remained brown, but pockets of early spring green-up had drawn bears into this small area. There had been recent sightings, but these tracks were about a week old and I found no fresh sign. I have searched far and wide in this area but have yet to see a bear on the Front—and yet to photograph one. Along with exploring, I've had to ask a lot of questions.

Along the Front, from Antelope Butte ▶

The Rocky Mountain Front is where the mountains meet the plains. Adjacent to Glacier National Park to its southeast, the Front is an integral and unique piece of the Northern Continental Divide Ecosystem. In general, the grizzlies are bigger here than anywhere else in the lower forty-eight states, and most of the females have larger litters and a faster reproductive rate. Bears here typically emerge earlier from their dens and gain weight quicker than others in Montana and Wyoming. This is not a dense population of grizzlies. They travel extensively and are widely dispersed. Although thousands once roamed the west, these shy and wary bears of the Front are among the few remaining grizzlies to thrive in these low, rolling grasslands.

When springtime beckons, grizzlies take advantage of early emerging succulent forbs, grasses, and sedges. They have also learned to seek out livestock carrion, which provides considerable calories. This may sound unnatural, but these are the same plains that used to support seemingly endless herds of bison, and the bears are adapting to present-day circumstances. Seasonal natural feeding patterns include consumption of insects, biscuit-root, and buffalo berries in the early summer along with heavy utilization of chokecherries through August and Sep-

tember. A bumper crop of chokecherries significantly enhances a bear's fall diet. Some grizzlies have been known to travel twenty miles or more east of the mountains, outside the Federal Grizzly Bear Recovery Zone, to feed on thorny buffalo berries in the fall. In poor years for berries and cherries, bears often move to alternative food sources such as oats, wheat, apples, and plums. Grizzlies are actually expanding into former bear country when they extend their home ranges farther to the east in search of food.

The trail to survival here often leads to lower-elevation private lands. These areas contain some great bear habitat, and the influx of grizzlies could increase in the coming years. In order to make a living on private land, some bears become habituated, which in this case means that bears become comfortable around ranches. Some of the habituated bears are nocturnal and rarely seen by people. A small percentage of these individuals become conditioned to nonnatural food attractants. Grizzlies have caused problems with sheep, pigs, grain, cattle, beehives, and poultry and have been known to enter barns to obtain horse feed. Young bears are frequently the culprits, and when trouble escalates the troublemaker is usually moved or destroyed.

Landowners in this area are now living with grizzlies, and they are wise to

do everything possible to minimize the availability of whatever attracts the bears. But even if they do, there are no guarantees. Bears are resourceful and opportunistic. Human tolerance is crucial, but problem grizzlies can make life difficult.

Local opinion and attitudes toward the grizzly along the Front are a mixed bag. At times, grizzlies have been observed walking among herds of cattle without reacting. Some folks see the bears as a nuisance and a threat to their livelihoods. Many others feel lucky to live in wild country and feel that losses due to predators are an expected part of the natural order they love. The Montana Department of Fish, Wildlife, and Parks (MDFWP) has invested a great deal to develop preventive measures and educate the local communities about how to live with the great bear. The preventive measures include extensive use of electric fences to keep bears away from domestic livestock. In addition, an innovative carcass redistribution program has helped to reduce conflicts between bears and humans while deterring some bears from becoming habituated to the ranch environment. The crux of this plan is to collect cattle and sheep carcasses from ranch boneyards each spring before the bears move in. This carrion is moved to remote sites within wildlife management areas that remain closed to the public

▲ *Highway 287, south of Choteau*

until May 15. Thus, the bears can feed in these areas without human disturbance and as a result may be less inclined to investigate private lands. To further minimize conflicts, hunters and campers are now required to carry bear-resistant food-storage containers in all adjacent national forest lands.

In recent times, along with the MDFWP management of areas on the Front, protection of bears and bear habitat has been significantly enhanced through land acquisitions by organizations such as the Nature Conservancy. Concerns remain regarding future road building, logging, subdivision development, and mechanized recreation along with the major threat of natural gas development, all in current grizzly habitat. The Federal Grizzly Bear Recovery Zones, where bear protection and conservation are given the highest priority and industrial activity is generally not allowed, were established twenty to thirty years ago on the basis of where bears were at that time. A lot has changed since then, with grizzlies moving well beyond the outdated Recovery Zone boundaries. These zones are proving to be inadequate to accommodate the changing needs of a viable bear population. There will always be conflicts, but suitable habitat must be preserved if we are to ensure a future for these prairie grizzlies.

Two Springs in the Life of a Yellowstone Family

I t was a gray afternoon as the bears cautiously circled the passive bison near the edge of a small meadow. One cub rubbed its back on a thin lodgepole pine as mom warily swayed her head back and forth with her nose low to the ground in a protective mode. The two large bulls were preoccupied with grazing and hardly looked up until the cubs began reacting to them with a combination of curiosity and worry. They pranced around in circles and whined nervously. Finally, their mother sat down, then rolled onto her back into the nursing position, still looking directly at the bison the entire time.

All this commotion finally got the attention of the two bison. They became curious, and both bulls gazed intently at the enthusiastic and loud

◀ *Playing near Obsidian Creek*

suckling activity. Throughout the four-minute nursing session, the mother bear never took her eyes off of the huge ungulates. As a light drizzle began, the three bears ate grasses while slowly disappearing into the forest. This concluded a long day for me—ten straight hours watching this animated bear family.

From May 4 to May 10, 2001, I had the great fortune of more-or-less steadily watching these three bears along the road corridor for a total of fifty-six hours. Many tourists and photographers came and went, but I recognized this as a rare opportunity and decided to observe every possible moment of their activities. With all my years of viewing in so many ecosystems, I had never been able to do this with any other bears. I saw more of this family in May and June, and the following spring, 2002, I again watched steadily as the now third-year cubs made their way toward separation.

This female was well known in the northern region of Yellowstone as bear number 264. She wore an old, non-functioning radio collar and was adept at killing elk calves in the spring. Her first two sets of twin cubs did not survive, and she was about nine years old when I first saw her near Roaring Mountain with the spring cubs of her third litter, on June 9, 2000.

Spring 2001

May 4. The winter was mild, but unseasonably cool spring weather contributed to a late green-up. The bears were in a wet roadside meadow just north of Roaring Mountain, a domed thermal area that was a familiar landmark in the mother bear's home range. On this glorious sunny afternoon in Yellowstone country, I was happy to see that the cubs had survived their first full winter. I wasn't sure what the bears were eating, but all three were digging steadily. The two yearlings nursed late in the day, then took a casual walk up to a nearby bluff where the whole family sacked out on a snowfield.

This brief nap was followed by a spirited play session, with all three rolling and tumbling through the snow. They all looked healthy and it was wonderful to see a playful mother grizzly exuberantly enjoying the moment. They returned to the meadow and snacked on grass before crossing the road to the east. As darkness descended, the three bears looked like ghostly shadows as they broke into a dead run across the soft white, sandy face of Roaring Mountain, then disappeared over the top.

May 5. As a thick layer of clouds descended from the north in the early morning, the bear family was at it again, digging in the same mucky meadow. The mother meticulously picked through the mud, continuously rolling over fresh dirt with her long claws. Watching her care–fully, I realized that she was searching specifically for earthworms. Along the way she ingested insects, grasses, and miscellaneous grubs, but it became apparent that she was actually hunting worms. She lifted her head and slurped every worm she could find; the cubs did the same between wrestling bouts. All three bears had muddy snouts as they pulled and tugged each other around.

As the day wore on, they traveled to the north, eating assorted grasses and searching for other foods. The bears crossed the road several times and, a surprise to me, took only a couple of short naps. Their routine was rounded out by three nursing sessions that lasted about four minutes each, including the previously mentioned episode near the bison bulls.

May 6. After a clear and cold night, the bears arrived early at the "worm meadow." The mother bear continued to roll sod all morning long, eating roots and insects while carefully selecting worms. She actually seemed to be avoiding the green vegetation. In the afternoon they headed south through another meadow, then back to the east toward Roaring Mountain. During this traveling process, they crossed the road several times and rolled around in numerous patches of lingering snow. All three got a great workout but not much to eat. By the end of the day, mom had led her offspring on a long loop, ending up back in the same "worm meadow" digging up fresh soil.

May 7. It was clear and 27 degrees Fahrenheit with early morning frost. I found the bears foraging about two miles to the south near Twin Lakes. They meandered near the western edge of a big meadow, but their digging was not intense and this area didn't seem to be a productive food site. After a late morning nursing session, they traveled slowly back toward the road. The trio then walked north along the pavement, followed by a convoy of cars and a busy park ranger.

The bears were again unable to find any new productive food source, and it was no surprise when they returned to the familiar "worm meadow." Mom's nose was clean when they arrived, but it didn't take her long to get a snootful of mud. At one point she became irritated by a diesel engine, and the three bruins bolted up the hill. She surveyed the scene, then circled across some crusty snow, and within a few minutes they were back in the meadow. During the afternoon the cubs nursed, napped, foraged, and played. Taking only a few short breaks, the mother grizzly dug up worms for five and a half straight hours, ending at 7:30 in the evening.

May 8. The brilliant morning was sunny and warm, and the bears were in the same predictable spot. By now the "worm meadow" was so thoroughly excavated that it looked as though there were few new spots left to dig among the piles of fresh muddy soil. The larger male yearling was showing increasing independence as he foraged across the meadow from mom and his brother. The early worming session lasted over three hours, during which the family paid little attention to all the people lined up along the road.

By noon the bears began traveling steadily to the north. They ate grasses and dandelions along the way and took only brief respite to play in the sulphur water of Obsidian Creek. When the mother bear spotted an elk herd, she immediately broke into a dead run with the cubs following close behind. They chased the elk up a steep slope and disappeared into the snow-covered timber. It was a futile attempt. There were no calves in this herd. I then realized that, for the first time in four days, the bears were out of my sight.

The family apparently napped in the shade. They reappeared only an hour and a half later, resuming their northerly route while eating grass along Obsidian Creek. They crossed the road and casually approached three bison cows with

calves. The bison dashed out of the timber, but the mother bear took only a few quick steps toward them, then watched them run away. Bison are bigger and more belligerent than elk. For the most part, this mother bear showed little interest in bison herds and rarely pursued them, even though small bison calves seem to be extremely vulnerable.

Continuing to the north, the three bears crossed the road at the Grizzly Lake trailhead. All three stopped to scratch and rub various parts of their bodies on the bridge and signposts near the trail. They galloped playfully into an open meadow to the west, and the mom began some serious digging. This time she wasn't looking for worms. As the sky darkened and the rains came, she seemed to be digging deeper and with more intensity. Dirt was flying straight up from the big hole she was hollowing out. She paused often to scan the moist soil for escaping rodents. Although it is common grizzly behavior, this was the only time I saw this bear trying to dig up ground squirrels. She spent over two hours creating a huge excavation, but from my distant vantage point I could not tell how successful she was. The light was dim and bears were moving farther away when I finally called it a day after watching them for more than twelve straight hours.

May 9. On a cool, overcast morning, the bears foraged near the Grizzly Lake trailhead. The cubs were licking up insects after clawing them off rotted wood. It was still early when their northerly excursion resumed along the road corridor escorted by a convoy of vehicles. From a swampy island in Obsidian Creek, they all stopped and looked anxiously toward another loud diesel. At this very spot they would spend an important week next spring.

The bruins gradually moved north to an open meadow, where they spotted a bison herd of eight cows with two newborn calves. As the bears approached, the bison circled into a protective wall with the calves hidden in the middle, much like musk oxen react to arctic wolves. With an intent look, the mother bear seemed determined to test this herd as she began to stalk closer. The bison made a split-second decision and immediately galloped away in single file along the edge of the timber, with the two calves toward the front of the herd. Upon seeing the reaction of the healthy bison, the mother bear countered with another token effort while the larger cub continued the chase by himself before turning back.

The grizzlies' relentless northern movement continued all day, followed by a long motorcade. They finally made a definitive move across Indian Creek, then up and over a snow-covered ridge

far to the west. This energetic bear family traveled many miles on this day, and the "worm meadow" was far away.

After an absence of close to four hours, the bears reappeared about another mile north just below Swan Flats. They were eating biscuitroot along the park road in the driving rain. These bears were exploring new country and broadening their seasonal diet while biding time before elk calving.

May 10. It was sunny and cool as the bears dug biscuitroot all morning long far to the west. In the early afternoon they returned to the road and continued to move north. They spent a good part of the afternoon meandering through sagebrush looking for newborn elk, but it was still too early for calving. Auto traffic was increasing, more folks were observing this spectacle, but the bears were becoming less visible. At the end of the day they headed west through Swan Flats before disappearing over a distant hillside.

What an incredible seven days of observation. With dry weather offering sparse feeding opportunities, the resourceful mother bear searched out a wide variety of nutritional resources in a short period of time. She was a good teacher. The cubs routinely nursed three times a day and began to take longer naps as temperatures rose. The family often foraged near the road and crossed it at will. I never saw them show any aggression toward humans, though some folks did some pretty stupid things. Park rangers continuously performed an outstanding job controlling the crowds while safely allowing people to enjoy these rare observations. I saw these bears four more times during this spring.

May 19. The bright sunlight illuminated their thick winter fur as the three bears foraged early in the morning in a swampy creek. The mother bear was favoring her right front paw. My friend Steve Merlino said that she had been limping more severely the day before, but no one knew what happened to her. It must have been a new injury because she apparently had been moving well when seen the previous day. All three bears looked good physically, but mom was obviously missing her customary vibrant energy and slept a lot more than what I had observed as normal for her.

The trio continued their usual behavior of crossing the pavement several times, causing all kinds of traffic problems. Along the way they consumed grasses mixed with glacier lily flowers, and they once again stopped to scratch and chew on the old wooden Grizzly Lake bridge. As far as I could tell, they had not returned to the "worm meadow" routine. The limping mom led her cubs far to the west, where they grazed on a partially greened-up south-facing ridge. In the early evening the three bears disappeared into the shadows over the far horizon, and I did not see them again for quite a while.

June 6. When I next saw the bears, the bounce had returned to the mother's step. With the injury apparently healed, she was moving fluidly and seemed like her old self. So much time had passed since my last observation that I don't know how long the healing process took, but it was great to see her strong and healthy. I watched for over an hour as the three bruins searched for elk calves near Twin Lakes.

June 14. It was near dusk as the mother bear's powerful nose circled through the drizzle following the scent of fresh carrion. On a steep hillside, an adult male grizzly was guarding a carcass, probably an elk calf, as she drew near and then retreated. With cubs in tow, she boldly challenged several times from different angles, but the larger bear bluff-charged and would not back down. During one approach, the adult bears growled mouth

to mouth, from point-blank range, and I was surprised by how close mom brought her yearlings to potential danger. I didn't know how successful the mother bear had been at finding elk calves recently, but there was no doubt from her actions that she really wanted this meat. When she made her last attempt, the male would still not budge. After the bear family finally moved away, the cubs nursed in the fading light.

June 15. It was a cold morning as several cow elk pranced around nervously while the bear family prowled the forest. Suddenly an elk calf was sprinting along the ridgeline with the mother bear in hot pursuit. The gap between them narrowed as the calf weaved its way through the open timber, cut sharply downhill, then screamed its final breath as the mother grizzly took it down less than thirty yards from the road in the bright sunshine.

The bears fed for about forty minutes before retiring to a shady spot in the nearby charred woods. There wasn't much left of the calf, but about three hours later they returned to polish off the scraps before moving on. The three bruins playfully traveled into the dense forest during the heat of the day. This was to be the last time that I saw them this year.

Spring 2002

On the cool, brilliantly clear morning of April 29 at 5:45 A.M., the mother grizzly and her two-year-old male cubs were feeding on a bison carcass very close to the park road in Obsidian Creek. They had probably not been out of their den long, and all three looked strong and healthy, with the larger cub beginning to approach the size of his mother.

The carrion was mostly submerged, making it difficult for the bears to get at the prime meat. To complicate matters, the bruin family was uneasy feeding on a carcass that was less than fifteen yards from human activity. Each time the bears were able to extricate a big chunk, they carried it back to the wooded hillside above. Here they could eat in peace, then bury what was left for a later snack. Unfortunately for them, when they disappeared higher up in the timber for naps, two clever coyotes, including one with a noticeable limp, pilfered these unattended stashes.

At high noon the park service made an executive decision to move the dead bison out of the creek and farther from the road. They reasoned that the close proximity was dangerous for both bears and humans, and that this spring feast would be more accessible to the bears if it were up and out of the water. They used a manual pulley system anchored around a nearby tree to drag the carcass up onto

the dry bank above the creek about fifty yards from the road. The mostly intact bison appeared to be a two- or three-year-old with no fur left on the smooth discolored body, which had been submerged and preserved for a long time.

After the carcass had been repositioned, the bewildered bruins returned for their next meal around noon. They followed the fresh trail drag scent directly to the carrion while carefully sniffing the human footprints. The cubs began to feed cautiously while mom investigated the entire scene, piecing the story together with her powerful nose. When she was comfortable that the situation was safe, she joined her boys at the newly exposed food source.

For five days the bears gorged. They seemed impervious to both human activity nearby and typical changes in spring weather ranging from bright sunshine to heavy wet snow. The three bears rarely fed at the same time. Preparing them for their independence, mom would usually let one or both cubs feed first, then move in when they were finished. With the cubs so big, nursing sessions looked like a huge pile of vibrating fur. The siblings often wrestled vigorously in the snow, with mom sometimes joining the fray. The larger cub usually got the best of his smaller brother.

In typical grizzly style, mom buried the carcass with fresh duff and snow after each feeding, but often one of the cubs would quickly undo her handiwork for another snack. Sometimes she slept right on top of this mound of meat to keep the pesky coyotes away. I was not able to watch the bears continuously as I had the previous year; each day they disappeared up into the shady cover of nearby timber for several hours. Every time they returned to the site, the three large grizzlies would make a grand entrance, carefully sniffing and looking around as they approached the carrion.

May 3. By the afternoon, the well had about run dry. There was precious little meat left on the bison carcass. The family still seemed tightly bonded, and I wondered if and when mom would kick the guys out. Although this is the normal time, mother bears sometimes keep cubs for a third year.

In the early evening, the bears were turning over the sparse remains of the carcass like a giant flapjack as they munched on the neck and tried to procure every remaining morsel. Meanwhile, a lone dark grizzly was approaching from the south near the edge of a long meadow. He moved warily but purposefully and was somehow keyed in to what was happening. He saw the human gath-

ering and avoided it by choosing a route high above through the forest. When he was directly across the road from the carcass, the mother bear picked up his scent. With her nose circling the air, she looked around anxiously and stood a couple of times to sort things out, with the cubs copying her actions. The moment she pinpointed the direction of the intruder's odor, she turned away and retreated rapidly to the east, with cubs in tow, stopping several times to look back as they ran up the mountain through the wet snow in a matter of seconds. The trio was panting as they stopped to rest at a well chosen lookout point high above.

The new bear had his own agenda. He continued to the north, well past all

the human commotion, then made a bold move across the road. He leaped over the creek and headed directly uphill toward the three bears sitting at their snowy perch. The mother bear apparently realized he was coming and took the cubs farther uphill and out of my sight. The dark grizzly, moving like a shadow against the snow, reached the lookout and sniffed all around. Then, instead of pursuing the bear family any farther, he backtracked down toward the carcass.

The dark, lanky male was on full alert as he made a dramatic approach. The closer he came, the more careful he appeared to be. With long, deliberate strides he crisscrossed the hillside through the lower bank of trees while sizing up the situation. Once he made up his mind, there was no hesitation. He marched purposefully directly up to the carcass, grabbed the thick hide with his powerful jaws, and immediately began to drag it backward over the well-trampled crusty snow. He paused momentarily to regrip and look around a couple of times, but in a matter of seconds he had pulled the remaining flesh and bones farther from the road to the base of a tree. He fed in the shadows until dark as I watched, shaking from excitement. This was a rare observation.

May 4. It was a cold frosty morning as the wary bruin lurked in the shadows at the same spot I left him the previous evening. Although munching on only a few meager scraps, he had obviously guarded this pile of skin and bones all night long. Timing is everything. A few days earlier he could have been eating a substantial amount of meat.

Just before sunrise, he trudged uphill through the snow. He followed the scent of the bear family as they took refuge on the high bluffs above. I wondered if courtship was on his mind. He approached the bears and appeared to touch noses with the mother. The cubs huddled nervously together nearby. I watched closely, but the action was hard to follow as the bears moved through the timber. The two adults walked together over a high saddle, with the cubs following at a safe distance. As they all disappeared I thought this was it: she would be mating and booting out the cubs today.

Whatever transpired when all four bears were out of sight will remain a mystery. A while later the cubs and mother came back down the slope, her suitor nowhere in sight. The cubs frolicked happily as they followed mom back down toward the creek to the shifted carcass site. They sniffed and picked for about an hour, the larger cub aggressively smacking the naked rib cage around like a wild child checking out a new toy. At 10:30 in the bright sunshine, mom led them away. The feast was officially over and, from this point on, the daily routine would be completely different. In the next few days they would search far and wide in their quest for more calories.

May 5. In early morning the bears passed through the "worm meadow" but spent just an hour before moving on. Actually, only mom dug for worms. The cubs went for the wet greenery, eating mostly grasses and sedges. After spending several days here the previous spring, worms and vegetation just didn't measure up this time around. They crossed the road and then traversed the lower part of Roaring Mountain, a landmark these cubs knew very well by now.

Heading south to Nymph Lake, they chased a herd of cow elk futilely. One cow went crashing through the lake, then labored through the muddy shallows to safety. The smaller cub lagged far behind and seemed lost as he cried out frantically for mom. The three reunited and ambled slowly down to the lakeshore, where the young bears climbed on top of mom and suckled for over four minutes. This was the first nursing I had witnessed since the encounter with the adult male the day before.

As snow and heavy winds moved in, they traveled all the way south to the Norris Geyser Basin. By early evening, however, they had reversed their course, ending up back at the "worm meadow."

They had made a grand loop of well over eight miles. When the bears headed south they were west of the road, and on the return trip they stayed to the east. They covered both sides thoroughly in an apparent search for more carrion. The three bruins had expended a lot of energy without much to show for it. Mom waited patiently each time the cubs lagged behind. On this day she showed no indication that the separation from her offspring was close at hand. I left them at the "worm meadow" that night as blowing snow was covering their backs.

May 6. Heavy wet snow was accumulating as the three bears journeyed north, repeating their usual routine of paralleling and crossing the road whenever and wherever they pleased. Thanks to a narrow V–shaped opening through a stand of young lodgepole pines, I watched them munch on the ribs, skull, and legs of an old bison carcass for just over an hour. It wasn't much meat, but probably better than worms or grass. The cubs later took turns leaping across Obsidian Creek on their way to a familiar place.

In short order they approached the spot near Obsidian Cliffs where the male grizzly had stolen the carcass a few days earlier. The mother bear looked a bit edgy as she sniffed the entire area warily. She was teaching the cubs a valuable safety

lesson, and they copied her behavior. The investigation took about seven minutes before they continued northward.

Late in the afternoon all three bears were digging for pocket gophers within fifty yards of the road. The cubs seemed to be in their own world digging across the meadow from mom. She called them back a couple of times. One by one each cub would come over briefly, like a dog checking in with its master, then scamper away. The young bears were gaining independence, and they often seemed to be more eager for the final separation than their mother.

May 7. The bear family traveled to the eastern edge of Swan Flats through the blowing snow. Winding their way down to a significantly lower elevation, they went all the way around the east side of Bunsen Peak to Mammoth Hot Springs. According to documented evidence, the female grizzly had never traveled this far north. The weather had been wintry in Swan Flats and void of elk, but it was much milder down in Mammoth and elk were abundant. For the past few days, these bears had been constantly on the move, with mom giving the boys a thorough review of her home range while expanding the search for food.

She apparently made a good call, for they found an intact cow elk carcass along the Gardiner River. Unfortunately, this feast was very close to park service housing, and all hell broke loose, with the entire area put on red alert. Rangers were everywhere trying to monitor the bears' movements. There was serious concern about their proximity to the residences, school, and campground. The bears would be tolerated if they stayed out of trouble. After constantly observing this active bear family for nine straight days, I decided to take a break.

May 8–10. While I was away, the bears finished off the cow elk carrion in less than two days. They proceeded to stroll through the Mammoth school grounds while children were attending class. Having grown up in the Chicago area, it is hard for me to imagine grizzlies walking by the window during a math test or rudely interrupting a softball game at recess. The trio brazenly continued right up the main road, past the post office and hotel, then to the hot springs before heading back up toward Swan Flats and their traditional home range to the south.

Although no one I know actually saw it happen, the final separation apparently occurred on May 10. Two years earlier I had seen two yearling cubs kicked out in nearby Shoshone National Forest on May 9. I consider bears to be cubs as long as they are dependent on their mother. In my absence, the young bears had been transformed from cubs to sub-adults.

It may appear somewhat callous that, after diligently raising cubs for over two years and forming a close bond, a mother grizzly pushes them away and usually ends the relationship forever. This sounds like a short time, but when you stop to think about it, mother and cubs are literally together every second, twenty-four hours a day, seven days a week. How does this compare to a human mother who raises a child until, say, the age of eighteen? Which mother spends more time with her children? Of course the fact that grizzly cubs do not grow up with a father certainly alters the equation, but it's all food for thought.

May 11. In the early morning I saw the two sub-adults together in a familiar area near Obsidian Cliffs. This was the first full day on their own. The young bruins spent considerable time chewing on a very old carcass. They had walked past this meager carrion with their mother five days earlier without even slowing down to give it a sniff. The young bears found a few scraps but mostly chewed on bones and hide. Still, it seemed significant; this was likely their first substantial food since separating from mom.

The larger sub-adult traveled away as his brother stayed behind to crunch more bones. With the first bear about a mile ahead, his smaller sibling finally rose up and followed the exact same path. At different intervals, they each crossed the road and headed into the woods along power lines near the Solfatara trailhead, a familiar route frequently used by their mother.

May 12. The smaller sibling napped alone in the forest just north of Roaring Mountain. Within the first forty-eight hours on their own, the two young males had gone their separate ways. I don't know if it's abnormal for siblings to split up so quickly; in my experience they usually stay together for a while. In this particular case, the fact that the larger bear was always dominant and far more independent may explain the early parting of ways.

June 2–12. From my observations during this period, all three bears traveled alone in the same general home range. Each was finding plenty of elk calves, and they were all in great shape. Mom had taught her sons well; both became prolific calf hunters just like her. The bears were taking full advantage of the annual window of opportunity to obtain ungulate protein. This opportunistic behavior certainly bodes well for their survival.

A Well-Earned Break

Managing the two-year olds before she kicked them out must have been exhausting. Here mom takes a peaceful nap.

2003 Postscript

The mother bear showed up in the spring of 2003 without new cubs. It's easy to speculate but impossible to know the reasons. Nevertheless, it was disappointing. This beautiful bear was now twelve years old, in the prime of her life, and apparently in excellent shape. She traveled alone and covered a lot of territory, much more than if she had tiny cubs to look after. I never did see the two male offspring she had kicked out the previous spring, but this is not surprising. Males frequently travel great distances, whereas females often stay close to their mother's home range.

On the morning of May 17, she was being courted by a male suitor near a carcass they both had been feeding on. The larger bear followed her away from the carcass site as she laid down. When he approached closely, she got up and quickly moved away. This typical courting behavior was repeated a couple of times. Finally, the shy male reacted to a loud vehicle and exited the area over a high ridge to the west. The female briefly returned to the carcass, then bedded down nearby for the day. At the time, I hoped that these two bears had mated and she would have cubs next spring. Little did I know that these photographs would turn out to be the last I ever took of her.

On the evening of June 14, she was struck by a car in the southern end of her home range near Norris Campground. She was tranquilized and taken to a veterinary clinic in Bozeman. X-rays showed a broken back, and she was partially paralyzed. She was euthanized the next morning.

This was a sad ending to the life of a very special bear. It had been a wonder-ful privilege to watch her through the past few years, but her tolerance for people and her comfort level along the roadside corridor ultimately led to her demise. I thank her for all she taught me about grizzly bear behavior and for all the great pictures she allowed me to take. May she rest in peace.

Acknowledgments

To my lifelong friend Ron "Bagelman" Giangiorgi, thanks for the edits. It's been a long road. I'll take Wendy. To my great friend and trail partner, Tim Rubbert. We've learned so much together. This book would never have been possible without you. To Larry Aumiller, thanks for your generous help and for fighting the good fight. I have learned so much from great talks with Chuck Schwartz. Thanks Chuck. To Mike Madel, thanks for helping me on the Front. I have so much respect for what you are doing. Thanks to Steve Merlino for his friendship while we share the trails. Thanks to John Thomas for his honest, insightful editing and opinions, and for sticking with me. Special thanks to Ryan James Berman for the Thanksgiving bear. Thanks Smokey! The most special thanks go to my wife Ingrid for her love, patience, and support throughout this process.